m

D0707928

309646

The Third Pig Detective Agency

in

The Curds and Whey Mystery

Also in the series

The THIRD PIG DETECTIVE AGENCY

THE CURDS & WHEY MYSTERY

BOB BURKE

FRIDAY
BOOKS

The Friday Project
An imprint of HarperCollinsPublishers
77–85 Fulham Palace Road, Hammersmith, London W6 8JB

www.harpercollins.co.uk

First published in Great Britain by The Friday Project in 2010

A catalogue record for this book is available from the British Library

ISBN 978-0-00-736403-9

Internal design and typesetting by Wordsense Ltd, Edinburgh
Printed and bound in Great Britain by Clays Ltd, St Ives plc

To my parents, Bobby and Nancy,
from whom I got my love of reading

Contents

Contents

1

Along Came a Spider

Sometimes being a detective isn't all that easy. Actually it's never that easy. Case in point, my current client: a small lady with a big arachnid problem.

'Spiders?' I said, ushering the very pale and very frightened Miss Muffet to the nearest chair.

'Yes, spiders,' Miss Muffet nodded faintly, lips trembling. She looked to be teetering on the edge of a complete breakdown – and I didn't fancy being the one left cleaning up the shattered pieces from my floor afterwards.

'Spiders,' I said again, still trying to get my head around what she was saying. 'As in small, scuttling things with eight legs that build webs in unswept corners?'

'No Mr Pigg, spiders as in large, hairy creatures the size of poodles; spiders that eat small animals and build webs that fishing trawlers could use to haul in whales. I'm not talking about a few tiny money spiders here; I'm talking about thousands of these giant eight-legged monsters running amuck in my house. Imagine putting a breakfast on the table and then, when the guest goes to get his coffee, he comes back only to find that a tarantula or somesuch has made off with his bacon,' she said. 'And not only that, spiders terrify me; always have done. I hate them. I can't even sleep there any more I'm so frightened. It's playing merry hell with my business.'

'And what business would that be?' I asked.

'Oh, sorry, didn't I say? I do apologise. I'm the proprietor of the Curds and Whey Bed and Breakfast on Grimm Road. Maybe you've heard of it?'

I gave a rueful shake of the head.

'Ah well, never mind. It used to be very popular with visitors and was very highly thought of. Until this happened, business was extremely good. I had full occupancy. Now, not too many people are keen on staying there.' Fumbling in her bag she took out a tiny white handkerchief and began dabbing her eyes just as the tears began to trickle. 'The house has been in my family for generations,' she said between sobs. 'If I can't get this sorted I'll have to close down and sell it. I can't let that happen. That's why I've come to you.' She looked up at me. 'I need you to find out who's doing this; find out who's trying to put me out of business. Can you help me, Mr Pigg?'

Now I'm normally not one to refuse a pretty lady, but there was just one teeny problem; well, a fairly big problem actually: I didn't like spiders either. Scratch that, I hated them. They were one of two things that really terrified me (and no, I'm not about to tell you what the other is; I don't want you laughing at me). Just the thought of one of those hairy creatures scuttling across my trotter sent shivers up and down my spine, along my arms and down my legs, where they stopped for a moment to catch their breath before running back up again for a repeat performance.

Miss Muffet's dilemma meant I now had to do a careful juggling act: fear of spiders versus earning money to pay some long outstanding bills – and some of my bill collectors were of the type that had a baseball bat as part of their corporate uniform. After a brief, but brutal, mental struggle, earning money came out a clear winner, actively encouraged by blind greed and aided and abetted by sheer desperation – fear of spiders never stood a chance.

I stood up and extended my trotter. 'Miss Muffet, the Third Pig Detective Agency would be delighted to take on your case,' I said, trying not to show any hint of the anxiety that was developing into full-blown arachnophobia in my head.

The look of relief on her face convinced me I'd done the right thing.

'Oh that's wonderful, Mr Pigg. I knew I could count on you.'

We'll see how much you can count on me when funnel-web spiders start doing the tarantella up and down my back,

I thought, but, of course, I didn't say it out loud; I had an image to maintain, after all.

I walked my new client to my office door.

'I think the first thing we should do is to go and have a look at your building,' I said. 'Maybe we'll find some clues there.' I didn't really want to – for obvious reasons – but I had to start somewhere and the B&B seemed like a good place to kick things off, although if what she said was true I'd spend most of the time kicking off spiders.

'An excellent suggestion,' said Miss Muffet. 'There's no time like the present. My car is outside. Why don't I drive?'

On the way to Miss Muffet's B&B she gave me some more background.

'Well, when I was a young girl there was nothing I enjoyed more than eating my bowl of curds and whey on the tuffet in the back garden.'

Curds and whey? No, I'd never heard of it either. I wasn't sure what it actually was, but it didn't sound like something I'd like. Mind you, I had no idea what a tuffet was either.

Miss Muffet continued her story. 'One morning I was busily tucking in as usual when I heard a noise beside me. I looked over and there was this enormous spider hanging down – a really big hairy one – looking at me as if I was going to be his breakfast. It quite frightened the life out of me. I was so scared my bowl shot into the air and spilled all over me. It made quite a mess, and curds and whey are so difficult to get out of clothes. After that, I never really liked spiders again.'

I nodded occasionally as she told the story. I could understand where she got her fear of spiders from – that much was obvious – but how did that connect to the sudden plague of them that was apparently infesting her business premises – if it was infested at all. If she was that frightened of spiders, maybe she'd just seen one or two and overreacted. I know I probably would have.

I started asking the obvious questions.

'Miss Muffet, do you have any enemies; anyone with a grudge or who might want to put you out of business?'

'Oh no,' she said, after thinking about it for a moment. 'I'm sure I don't. Who could possibly want to do such a thing? I don't think I've ever had any problems with anyone.'

'Has anyone shown an interest in buying you out?'

'Well, I have turned down offers over the years, of course. It was always a lucrative business and people were forever looking to buy me out, but I always resisted.' She frowned as she remembered something. 'Mind you, there was one gentleman recently who did phone a number of times offering to buy the building. He was most persistent, but I kept on refusing. Eventually he stopped calling. I do remember because he had a strange, squeaky kind of voice.'

Motive, I thought to myself.

'And you have no idea who it might have been?'

'I didn't pay much attention, to be honest, and I never thought to ask for his name.'

She drove around a corner and onto a long street. 'Here we are, Grimm Road. I'm at the far end.'

Apart from yellow construction vehicles in the distance and a few cars parked outside some of the houses, the street itself seemed very quiet. But as I looked out of the window a most bizarre sight greeted me. Turning to Miss Muffet, I pointed to what I'd seen.

'Is that a...shoe?' I gasped in amazement.

Now I should point out that this wasn't just an ordinary shoe that someone had lost while running from the scene of the crime. This was a giant shoe; a shoe the size of the building my office was in. This was a piece of footwear that dwarfed all others into insignificance – a mega-shoe. As I gaped at it I thought I could see... 'Are those windows?' I asked.

'Hmm, pardon? Oh, yes,' replied Miss Muffet with a complete lack of interest. 'Those are probably windows.'

Considering what I was looking at, her response puzzled me. She was acting as if this was quite an ordinary event.

I nudged her gently. 'You don't seem particularly surprised at seeing what looks like a giant shoe at the end of your street.'

'Don't I?' she replied. 'Well, I do see it every day. It's the Shoe Hotel. It's been there for years. A little old lady lives in it. She runs it as far as I know.'

Now it began to make sense. I vaguely remembered reading about a series of themed hotels that had opened up all around the country over the past few years. This must have been one of them but, as themed hotels went, it was quite spectacular. It had been designed to look like a trainer – all white paint and blue stripes – and would never suffer from foot-odour. The huge entrance doors were where the (presumably very large) big toe would have been and the shoelaces were large plants that draped down along the walls. From the small number of cars in the car-park, business didn't appear to be too good. That was significant. More to the point, it was just possible that the owners mightn't take too kindly to competition from a local B&B and might be only too delighted to see it close its doors.

More motive.

I made a note to speak to this 'little old lady' on my way back.

'And you've never spoken to the owner of this hotel?' I asked.

'No, I don't even think I've ever met her. Ah, here we are,' Miss Muffet said as she pulled into the driveway of a large house. 'Well,' she said as she stopped the car and we got out, 'shall we take a look?'

From the outside the B&B didn't look particularly frightening. It was a three-storey brown brick building with white lace curtains in all the windows. Very homely indeed.

But was there something odd about those curtains?

'Miss Muffet, why do you have lace curtains on the outside of all your windows?' I asked.

The look she gave me suggested she might be having second thoughts about utilising my services as a detective. 'Those aren't curtains, Mr Pigg, they're webs.'

I took a second, closer look and, to my horror, I could see she was right. What I thought were curtains were in fact giant spider webs that covered all the windows from top to bottom. This lady hadn't been exaggerating. If the webs were anything to go by, she did have a major spider problem and probably some major spiders causing the problem. I wasn't at all sure I wanted to go inside now. In fact, I was thinking about turning around, running straight back to my office and hiding behind my desk until they went away.

Miss Muffet must have read my mind as she grabbed me by the arm and pulled me towards the door.

'It's okay,' she said gently. 'They tend not to be too active this time of the day. They mostly come out at night – mostly. We should be able to look around without being disturbed too much.'

I was disturbed enough already and I wasn't sure that I particularly wanted to look around the inside any more but, for such a slight woman, she was incredibly strong; she propelled me through the front door and into the lobby before I could change my mind.

Inside, it was as if the whole interior had been redecorated by someone from Haunted Houses 'R' Us. Huge strands of ghostly web hung over the stairs and all the furniture. Long wispy tentacles extended from the ceiling and drifted in the draught from the front door. One trailed across the side of my face. It felt like someone breathing gently on my cheek and I jumped in fright.

Miss Muffet laughed quietly. 'After a while you just learn to ignore it.'

As I looked around I could see that, just like she said, there didn't appear to be too many active spiders. I'd never heard of them taking afternoon naps before, but I was glad they did. Spider siesta meant they weren't going to bother me – for which I was grateful. I could see large dark shapes huddled up in some of the webs but, understandably, I didn't examine them too closely. The last thing I wanted to do was to wake any of them up.

Miss Muffet gave me a guided tour, but apart from all the webs there wasn't much to see. The ground floor comprised a large dining room, a guest lounge, a small reception area, Miss Muffet's office and the kitchen. The rest of the building was taken up by bedrooms. Other than the webs there certainly wasn't anything obvious in the way of clues and I'm a very observant pig – I spotted the giant shoe hotel, didn't I? By the same token, I was keeping a very close eye out for any spiders that might suddenly awake and decide they wanted to play with me.

As I wandered around the house a couple of things began to bother me – other than the spiders. Apart from the little ones that you'd find in any ordinary house, spiders weren't too easy to come by. So where did the thousands of spiders that had taken over Miss Muffet's house come from? Someone must have supplied them – and they were probably very specialised, so certainly weren't picked up off the shelf from alongside the tins of beans and cereals in the local supermarket. That was certainly something to follow up. It was time to talk to my informant – although, if past history was anything to go by, he'd barely be able to inform me of his name let alone give me any useful information.

The other thing that nagged at me was Miss Muffet's mention of guests. It meant she must still have had some staying in the house. So why exactly were they staying? Unless they were keen students of spiders there was no sane reason to stay in the B&B – especially with a lovely, shiny, shoe-shaped hotel just up the road.

'How many people are actually staying here at the moment?' I asked.

Miss Muffet did a quick calculation. 'Nine, I believe.'

'And they've shown no indication of wanting to leave because of your infestation?'

'No, not at all. In fact, I haven't received a single complaint,' she said proudly.

Now that struck me as more than a tad suspicious. For someone to want to stay in a house infested with spiders, they'd need a particularly good reason – a reason that might just be connected with the case – especially when there were so many other places to stay.

'Can I have a list of your current guests and all your employees?' I asked.

'Of course, but surely you don't believe any of them are involved,' Miss Muffet replied, a bit naively I thought.

'At the moment I'm not ruling anything out,' I said, grabbing for the usual clichés as she reached behind the reception desk and opened the register.

'Here you are,' she said. 'Nine guests: Mr and Mrs Jack Spratt, Queenie Harte, John B. Nimble, Licken and Lurkey, William Winkie, Pietro Nocchio and, lastly, Thomas Piper.'

'I'll have to speak to all of them; can you arrange that?' I said, then I focused on what she'd actually told me. 'Did you say Licken and Lurkey?'

'Oh, yes, indeed, they're a rather entertaining team.'

She might have been a savvy businesswoman but her taste in entertainment was clearly lacking. Licken and Lurkey were a cabaret act that had been run out of every theatre in town – and in most other towns in the county as well. They marketed themselves as the WORLD'S MOST RENOWNED AND ENTERTAINING COMEDY DUO (their capitals, not mine, I hasten to add), but they were about as entertaining as having boils lanced. I also had history with them. Back in the days before becoming the WORLD'S MOST RENOWNED AND ENTERTAINING COMEDY DUO, they had toured the country as the WORLD'S

MOST ASTOUNDING MAGIC ACT – which had been neither magic nor astounding. I'd been asked to investigate a series of dove disappearances and had discovered that they all coincided with a performance by the despicable duo. As their act included the standard 'dove from a hat' trick and as the dove escaped during each performance, never to be recaptured, they had to find new ones for every show. Did I mention they weren't too bright? I hadn't realised they were still in town, but they'd be first on my list of interviewees as, from past experience, they were a pair who weren't too worried about getting their talons dirty.

2

There Was an Old Lady

Having assured Miss Muffet that I was on the case and following a specific line of enquiry (yes I know, it wasn't exactly true, but it got me out of spider central), I called for a taxi and made my way back into town. As we drove past the giant Shoe Hotel I asked the driver to pull in for a moment. No harm in asking a few questions, I thought.

Inside, the hotel was sparkling clean and, thankfully, there wasn't a cobweb to be seen. I approached reception and asked to speak to the manager. The receptionist looked at me strangely – I suppose they didn't get pigs in every day – but when I showed her my ID, she relaxed a little and ushered me into a small office. Behind a large desk sat a tiny old lady composed, it seemed, entirely of wrinkles. She looked like an elephant's knee. As I entered she stood up and pottered around to me. She was so decrepit it seemed to take her hours.

'Mr Pigg,' she said in a wavering voice, 'I'm Mrs Sole. How may I be of assistance?' She spoke so quietly I could barely hear her. With what seemed like an enormous effort, she waved me to a chair and, several lifetimes later, pottered back to her seat once more.

'Mrs Sole, I'm hoping you can help me. I'm investigating an infestation of spiders in the Curds and Whey B&B down the road, so I'm speaking to all other hoteliers in the area to see if they've been having similar problems.' It wasn't the most original of approaches and her reply confirmed that she'd seen through it straight away.

'And you're wondering if I may have something to do with it as I'm the only competition in the vicinity,' she whispered, some of the wrinkles forming what might have been a smile. 'Well, Mr Pigg, let me tell you about this hotel. We may not have too many cars in our car-park but you've probably noticed, being a detective, that they are all very expensive cars.' I hadn't, in fact, but nodded my head in agreement so as not to give the game away. 'You see we cater for the more...ah...discerning client at the upper end of the market. At the present time, Mr Humpty Dumpty, whom I'm sure you've heard of, occupies the penthouse suite and some business partners of Aladdin's have taken over the entire second floor. So, you see, that old building at the other end of the street really doesn't offer anything in the way of competition.'

She was certainly making a convincing argument. If Grimmtown big-shots like Dumpty and Aladdin used this hotel, then Mrs Sole wasn't going to worry too much about putting Miss Muffet out of business. Besides, she seemed like a sweet, kind old lady. Surely she wouldn't have been spiteful enough?

'Well, anyway, thank you for your time. You've been most helpful.' As I stood to leave, the phone rang.

'Excuse me a moment, won't you,' said Mrs Sole and lifted the receiver. It was like watching a weightlifter doing the clean and jerk. She was having so much difficulty I was almost tempted to hold it for her when she finally managed to get it to her ear. 'Yes, this is she,' she whispered into the mouthpiece. There was a brief silence, then Mrs Sole exploded.

'WHAT DO YOU MEAN THEY'LL BE LATE?' Suddenly she wasn't such a retiring old lady any more. 'IF THOSE FLOWERS AREN'T DELIVERED IN THE NEXT HOUR, YOU WON'T HAVE A JOB. UNDERSTAND?' There was a brief pause. 'AND YOUR BOSS TOO.' Her voice rose a few more decibels. 'AND I'LL HAVE YOU RUN OUT OF TOWN; YOU'LL NEVER DO BUSINESS IN GRIMMTOWN AGAIN. UNDERSTAND?' Another pause then she changed back into 'nice old lady' again, as if by magic. It was terrifying to watch. 'They'll be here in ten minutes? Why, that's wonderful. Thank you so much.'

She heaved the phone back in its cradle and turned to me, smiling sweetly once more.

'You just can't get good staff any more,' she said.

I just nodded. I was shell-shocked and wanted to be out of the hotel before she lost her cool again – perhaps with me – and it wasn't something I thought I'd particularly enjoy. Backing away towards the door I waved faintly at her and thanked her again.

'Not at all,' she whispered. 'I've quite enjoyed our little chat. We must do it again sometime.'

Not in a million years, I thought, as I raced across the lobby and back into the taxi. Instructing the driver to get us out of there as fast as he could, I slumped down in the back seat and considered what I'd seen. Clearly, Mrs Sole wasn't quite the demure lady she appeared. That having been said, she was probably right about not caring about Miss Muffet's business. She may have been as nuts as a squirrel's winter store, but I didn't see her as the primary suspect in this particular case. It really didn't make any business sense for her to see the Curds and Whey B&B as a threat.

I needed to do some further investigating and the spiders seemed like the next best thing to follow up on. Who could have supplied them? It's not as if they were something you'd order every day. I could even envisage the conversation in the pet shop:

'Do you sell spiders?'

'Yes, sir. We do most species. Would you like one or a pair?'

'Well, I'd like ten thousand actually.'

'Well, I can manage about twenty – maybe thirty at a pinch.'

Eventually every pet shop in Grimmtown would have been emptied of spiders and they still wouldn't have had enough – whoever 'they' might actually be.

It was the best (and only) lead I had right now.

Back in the office, I gathered my team (okay an ex-genie named Basili – who couldn't do magic any more – and a little boy called Jack Horner) together and explained the current case. Jack seemed very interested in the spiders. He seemed to think that a house full of them was cool for some reason.

'If I was looking for spiders, how would I go about it?' I asked him.

'Pet shop.'

'Well, that much I'd worked out for myself. Now supposing I wanted a couple of thousand of the critters; tarantulas, black widows, all the big guys.'

Now I had his attention.

He mulled it over for a second. 'Well, not too many of the local shops would be able to supply that many.'

I noted the use of the phrase 'not too many'.

'Best guy to talk to would be the Frogg Prince. He specialises in reptiles, spiders, that sort of thing. If anyone could do it, he'd be your man – I mean frog. I got my gerbil off him; he's called Fred.'

I assumed he was talking about his pet and not the owner of the store.

'And where is this Frogg Prince likely to be found exactly?'

Twenty minutes later I was talking to an enormous frog dressed in a grey pinstripe suit. Had I not been a pig myself it might have been a bizarre experience, but in Grimmtown you tended to meet all shapes and sizes – and creatures.

Theodore Frogg was the owner of Frogg Prince Pets and apart from a tendency to *ribbit* occasionally when talking, he was relatively normal – or at least as normal as a frog in a suit can be.

'Ah, yes, Mr Pigg, we did *ribbit* get an order that exhausted our entire supply of arachnids and we still *ribbit* had to provide more.'

'Arachnids?' He'd lost me.

'Spiders dear boy, *ribbit*, spiders. Yes, it presented us with quite a challenge I can *ribbit* tell you. But we managed it.' He glowed with pride, but then again it might just have been the natural state of his skin – it was quite shiny.

I was getting that tingly feeling that I usually got when a case finally started to come together.

'Who ordered the spiders?' I asked.

'Well, strange to relate, *ribbit*, it was a most unpleasant person indeed; very small, very green, extremely smelly and with a large wart on the end of his nose. Spoke in a kind of squeaky voice. He was somewhat bedraggled and quite offensive – but he did pay in advance so I *ribbit* didn't ask too many questions. In any event, I didn't want to refuse as he had two rather large creatures with him and I *ribbit* found them quite intimidating. I got the distinct impression they weren't about to take "no" for an answer.'

This was getting stranger by the minute, but the reference to speaking in a squeaky voice hadn't been lost on me. I'd have laid money that this was the same creature that had offered to buy the B&B from Miss Muffet.

'Creatures? What kind of creatures?'

'Large grey creatures dressed in *ribbit*, well, very little actually. They did *ribbit* rather frighten me, I must say.'

Large grey creatures; probably Trolls. Someone was certainly making sure the Frogg Prince wasn't going to renege on this particular deal.

'And they just instructed you to deliver them to the Curds and Whey B&B?'

'Good heavens, no. I just had to organise the acquisition of the spiders. They said they'd *ribbit* collect.'

'And you didn't think that this was at all suspicious?'

'Not at all, no. I just assumed they were scientists and needed them for research.'

That certainly wasn't likely. One small, green, smelly person and two trolls were about as far from science as you could get. 'And I assume they paid cash up front?'

Frogg nodded guiltily, knowing he'd been rumbled.

'So once you had the spiders, how did you contact them?'

Mr Frogg rummaged around in his wallet. 'They left me a number. Here it is.'

He handed me a piece of paper with some scrawled digits on it. It looked like a mobile phone so probably wouldn't lead to anything, but I had to follow it up anyway. 'And how did they collect the merchandise?'

'They came in a big *ribbit* truck and loaded everything into it.'

I thanked Mr Frogg and walked back onto the street. As I did, a large transport truck, with an equally large bulldozer on its trailer, passed by. A yellow bulldozer, I noticed idly.

Yellow!

Construction yellow!

My mind began to make the connections and I finally began to do some serious detecting.

Construction workers – or more to the point, construction trolls – like the ones that tended to frequent Stiltskin's Diner of an evening, and very like the ones I'd seen working near the B&B.

Small, green, smelly person! Could only be an orc. And who employed all the orcs in Grimmtown? Ah, now that wasn't so good. That was someone I particularly didn't want to upset if I wanted to keep all my body parts intact.

Things were beginning to make sense. Someone wanted Miss Muffet out of business all right – but that someone wasn't running a rival hotel; oh no, that someone wanted her out because she was in the way of something much bigger. It was all becoming very clear. Now all I had to do was prove it. I needed to pay a visit to a building site – and make sure I wasn't caught in the process.

3

Follow the Yellow Brick Road

B uilding sites are difficult to find your way around at the best of times. Add in some night, a sprinkling of rain, a generous helping of mud and not only are they difficult, but they become downright unpleasant. The ground that has already been excavated becomes very slippery. Pools of cold, dirty water lie in wait for the unwary pig and, if the pig is very unlucky, there are large holes in the ground just waiting for him to fall into.

This particular building site was about a mile from Miss Muffet's place. Huge hoardings announced that a new motorway, coming soon, would provide access to Grimmtown for countless commuters, blah de blah de blah. It was the usual **PR** doubletalk. Of more interest was the name of the construction company involved in this wondrous feat of engineering: The Yellow Brick Road Construction Company looked to be doing this particular job. Then again, as it was owned by Edna, the Wicked Witch of the West Side, an old sparring partner of mine (to put it as euphemistically as I could), the YBRCC did most building jobs around Grimmtown. To an outsider, it probably seemed amazing how they always managed to get the big building deals. As any insider would tell you, they greased politicians' palms, encouraged planners to 'share' any competitive quotes and generally bullied any other prospective contractor out of business. If they were doing this job and Miss Muffet was in the way, then chances were she wouldn't be in the way long. More to the point, if the spider strategy didn't work then they'd probably find something a tad more imaginative to encourage her to sell up.

I knew Edna of old and knew she wasn't a woman to be trifled with, especially where money or power was concerned. She was also a woman who didn't let much get in the way of achieving whatever her current objective was, so I had to tread very carefully indeed if I wasn't to become a permanent part of the motorway foundations. Not that I wasn't treading carefully already. Not only was I trying not to ruin my clothes, I was trying to make sure I didn't break any legs, arms or other vital parts of my body by suddenly falling into one of those previously mentioned large holes.

I figured if there was any information about the building work, like plans or drawings, it'd be in the construction hut. I could just about make it out in the distance, a small, cheap prefab mounted on blocks. I squelched my way towards it, unsure of what was ahead of me. In order not to alert any security I had decided not to use my torch – a decision I was now regretting as it seemed that every large puddle on the site lay between me and my destination and I was stepping into each one in succession.

Eventually – cold, wet and muddy up to my knees – I arrived at the hut. I listened carefully at the door and, when I didn't hear any obvious sounds from inside, very carefully picked the lock and slid in. Considering my history at picking locks, it was surprisingly easy. Ensuring the window blinds were closed, I was finally able to flick on my torch and a pencil-thin beam of light swept the room.

In fairness, it didn't take much in the way of detecting skills to figure out what was going on – the plans were in plain sight, tacked to one of the walls. It would have taken a pretty poor detective to miss them. They confirmed the construction of a new ring road around Grimmtown and the road ran straight through where the Curds and Whey B&B currently stood. Was it any wonder someone wanted her out? If they had been foolish enough to start work on the road without ensuring beforehand that all the land could be built on, then I could understand their urgency. Every day that the road couldn't go through Miss Muffet's house was another day of unnecessary costs to the construction company and, if I knew Edna, she wouldn't take too kindly to any unnecessary costs – or indeed any costs at all usually.

Now that I had the information I needed it was time to disappear. Unfortunately, that looked like it was going to be a futile wish as, just when I was getting ready to open the door, I heard noises from outside the hut. I could tell they were gnomes from the growling half-animal sounds they made, so it probably meant that Edna's security had been doing their rounds and were coming back to base – a base I was currently occupying and didn't seem to have anything remotely large enough to hide a pig in. I had a quick – and admittedly extremely optimistic – glance at some filing cabinet drawers, but had to concede that I'd barely get my legs into one of them, let alone the rest of my body. Once the gnomes opened the door they could hardly miss me and, stupid though they were, they would certainly have enough sense to realise I wasn't supposed to be there. Heaving a long and resigned sigh, I knew there was only one thing for it. I braced myself against the wall opposite the door and waited.

I didn't have to wait long.

'Check hut?' muttered the first gnome.

'Yeah, we check,' agreed the second.

'Got key?'

'No, you got key.'

'No, me not got key. You got key.'

At which point there was a minor scuffle, during which one or the other (it was hard to tell which) found that they did have the key after all.

The Curds and Whey Mystery

Seconds later peace had broken out and the door opened cautiously. Two unkempt gnomes entered, preceded by their smell. As soon as they were in view, I let out a loud roar and rushed straight at them. It was no contest; a fine specimen of prime ham landing on two weedy security guards, who were already terrified at finding a very large and very angry creature in a hut that had most definitely been empty the last time they'd looked.

The impact took all three of us back out through the door and into a pool of mud on the ground beyond. Fortunately, the gnomes broke my fall, so they took the brunt of the landing as well most of the mud. From the cracking noises I heard it was obvious that my fall wasn't all they'd broken. As I struggled free, one of them sank his teeth into my leg and I roared in pain.

'Pig,' howled the gnome to his companion as he recognised the taste. 'Not monster; pig.'

As I've already mentioned, gnomes are quite stupid. In this instance they were stupid enough not to realise they'd been injured, but not so stupid that they didn't recognise that their attacker was a pig. Figuring I was easier meat (possibly literally) now that they knew I wasn't a creature of the night, they seemed a bit more positive about chasing me. Staggering to their feet they lurched after me. Although I had the benefit of a fully working body, they had the advantage that they knew the terrain, so while I splashed my way across a sea of mud, they took drier, less slippery paths and slowly began to close in on me.

I have to say I was, by now, getting just a tad concerned as I was totally lost, had no idea where I was going and couldn't see my way off the building site. Meanwhile, Tweedledumb and Tweedledumber were gradually getting nearer – moving towards me in straight and presumably dry lines while I blundered around in circles getting muddier and wetter.

'That's 'im over there,' shouted one suddenly, and he scuttled in my direction.

I panicked and began to run. Heedless of where I was going, my only thought was to put as much distance between me and them as I possibly could.

Through the darkness I was just able to make out a small mound of earth. Maybe I could hide behind it. Figuring that it was a better option than wandering aimlessly around a building site in the dark, I dived over it. To my horror I found that, rather than landing on the ground beyond... well...remember those large holes I was talking about earlier? That's what was at the far side of that little mound. Bracing myself for impact, I landed with a resounding splash into a large pool of dirty water that covered me from head to toe in cold, wet mud. No need to worry about keeping clean now, but from what I could hear of my pursuers I was now so well camouflaged that they had problems finding me. They probably figured I was just another heap of mud.

'Where he go?' said one.

'Dunno,' said the other. 'Maybe he escape.'

'No, he still here. Me heard big splash.'

Clearly my new muddy ensemble allowed me to blend in perfectly with my surroundings. It may have been freezing and mucky but at least it was keeping me safe.

After a half-hearted search, the two gnomes gave up looking for me, finished their patrol and headed back to the hut. Rather than continue to wander in confusion around a dark building site, I chose to remain hidden where I was – cold and wet – until daylight. As soon as the skies began to lighten and I could see my way, I sneaked out of the building site and made my way home for a long, warm and much needed shower.

4

Revenge Is a Dish Best Served with Bacon

ater that morning – clean, dry and smelling so much nicer – I considered my options. I knew who was trying to frighten Miss Muffet out of business and I knew why. Now all I had to do was convince one of Grimmtown's most notorious criminals to back off and leave my client alone. I was more than a bit apprehensive as, even though I had something over Edna, she was a woman who didn't like to be crossed, especially if it involved her losing money – and I was quite certain that, in this instance, it would.

I required a plan; I needed it to work and, above all, I needed it fast. But I was stumped. Yes, the great detective didn't know what to do. As I sat at my desk waiting for inspiration, I had a quick read of the front page of our daily newspaper, the *Grimmtown Times*. The headlines were of the usual type:

Dumpty Wins Citizen of the Year for Third Year Running.
Grimmtown Goblins Reach Regional Finals.
Tuffet's Historic Status Confirmed by Local Archaeologist.
Mother Goose Wins Libel Case. Ugly Duckling Must Pay Damages.
Troll Finally Evicted from under Bridge. No More Tolls for Locals.

As I scanned them, the germ of a plan began to formulate. The more I thought about it, the more excited I became. I might just be able to pull this one out of the hat after all. I could even see my own headline: 'Third Pig Saves the Day – Miss Muffet Stays.' I grinned to myself and called Miss Muffet. It was time to swing into action.

An hour later Miss Muffet and I were standing outside the front door of Edna's massive mansion. It was a very impressive house indeed – more like a palace. Built completely out of white marble, it stood at the top of a hill overlooking the rest of Grimmtown. If I were rich, it was just the kind of house I'd like to have. Unfortunately, I had to make do with a grotty flat that gave a great view of the local abattoir. It didn't really compare.

The massive door in front of us swung inwards and one of Edna's personal bodyguards, a large silverback gorilla in a tuxedo, stuck his head out for a look. There was a short pause while it tried to figure out where it had seen me before, followed by a spark of recognition and a very impressive accelerated leap backwards, his eyes bulging in fear. Miss Muffet was visibly impressed. If I could scare a gorilla like that, I was clearly the right man for the job. I neglected to tell her that, as a result of my last encounter with Edna and her goons, I had a protective spell placed on me. Any time one of the gorillas approached me, it began to shrink. By the time it reached me it was usually the size of a puppy and not in a position to do much by way of damage. It was a kind of magical restraining order and was the only thing that was allowing me to brazenly confront Edna in her lair. Well, would you want to take on two fully grown gorillas with bad attitude, bad breath, bad posture and bad dress sense – and that's on top of all the other representatives of the criminal brotherhood that hung around in Edna's? I'd met some of them before, during my last visit here, and it hadn't ended well for quite a few of them. I'm sure they'd relish the prospect of another visit from me.

While the gorilla disappeared – presumably to announce my arrival – another, less impressive denizen of the house came out to see who was at the door. There was a short pause while it too tried to figure out where it had seen me before, followed, eventually, by another spark of recognition. It seemed to be the day for them.

'Pig here,' he shouted over his shoulder.

'Pig from last night?' came a reply from inside.

'Yeah. Maybe now we sort him out,'

The first gnome rushed at me and then goggled in surprise as he was suddenly grabbed by the neck and swung sideways. As his colleague ran out after him, he suffered the same fate. Both had failed to notice the two rather large creatures that stood on either side of the door. We hadn't come unprepared.

'Ah, you haven't met my associates, Mr Lewis and Mr Carroll,' I said, indicating the two massive ogres each of whom was dangling a gnome by the neck. Well, did you really think I was just going to walk into Edna's unprepared – magic restraining order or not? I'm not that stupid.

Both gnomes gurgled something which might have been, 'Please let us go, we are in considerable discomfort,' or might just as easily have been, 'We are delighted to make the acquaintance of these two large gentlemen you cleverly brought with you as protection.' It was hard to tell, but one thing was for sure, they weren't in a position to do anything threatening to either Miss Muffet or me. Mr Lewis and Mr Carroll had that kind of effect. Each was over eight feet tall and, when squeezed into a black tuxedo, looked very intimidating indeed. I had brought them with me exactly for this kind of situation.

'Gentlemen, I think you can put them down. I don't believe they will be too much trouble from now on.'

Both gnomes tried to nod their agreement – but it's difficult to nod when your neck is being tightly clenched by a hand the size of a beach ball.

At my signal, both of them were dumped unceremoniously on the ground, where they lay in a gnomish heap, blubbering and trying to skulk away. I almost felt sorry for them – almost.

'Okay chaps, let's go find Edna.' The ogres squeezed through the door after us as we entered the house. As we made our away across the wide lobby, gnomes and orcs scattered in all directions, clearly not wanting to engage our group in any form of physical contact. I can't say I blamed them; my minders had that effect on people.

Edna's office wasn't too difficult to find simply because it was the room that the loud voice screaming, 'Who the blazes is interrupting my telephone call?' was emanating from. Looking a lot braver than I actually was, I took a deep breath and swung open the office door.

Edna sat behind an ornate desk with a phone to her ear. As soon as she saw me she told whoever was on the other end of the line that she'd call them back and hung up.

'Well, well, well, if it isn't Harry Pigg, the world's greatest detective,' she sneered. Then she saw Miss Muffet. 'And look who's with him: Little Miss Muffet. Hey darling, seen any spiders lately?'

I decided that cutting to the chase was the best option. 'Okay Edna, we know what you're at,' I said. 'And just so as you know, Miss Muffet isn't selling, regardless of how you try to intimidate her.'

'Why, Harry, I have no idea what you're talking about. Why would I want to buy that tatty B&B? Tourist accommodation isn't really my style.'

'No, but building roads is,' I replied. 'I've seen the plans. Without Miss Muffet's house, your construction company can't complete that new motorway. It'll be very bad for your reputation if you don't; not to mention all the money you'll lose if the work doesn't finish on time. Maybe that's why you're trying to encourage her to sell up.'

To my surprise, Edna didn't seem at all worried that she'd been rumbled; in fact, she seemed unusually calm. An uneasy feeling started to gnaw at my stomach – and it wasn't because of what I'd had for breakfast. Something was very wrong here.

'From what I hear, things aren't too good in the local B&B trade. Strikes me that an infestation of spiders would be really bad for business,' she said. 'I could even see the health inspectors closing the premises down. Now that would be unfortunate. But if it did happen, I'd certainly feel for the owner. Losing your business is a terrible thing.'

'Indeed, but, of course, if it did close and you did buy it, you couldn't knock it down so your motorway could go through.'

'Sorry, Pigg, I have no idea what you mean.'

'Come on Edna, cut the nonsense. This is me, Harry Pigg, you're talking to. I know exactly what you're at.'

'No, I don't think you do,' Edna said, with the faintest of smiles beginning to smear her singularly unattractive features.

I decided to play my trump card so as to avoid an unnecessary 'oh yes I do', 'oh no you don't' conversation.

'Look, let's not play around any more. You want Miss Muffet out so you can build your road; she's not moving, so you're trying to scare her, but I've discovered that no matter what you do, you won't be able to demolish her house because...' – I whipped a copy of the day's newspaper out of my pocket like a cheap magician pulling a rabbit from his hat – 'tuffets are protected under Grimmtown bye-laws. They won't let you touch that house.' I was almost tempted to follow it with a ta-dah and a cheesy bow, but I figured Edna mightn't take too kindly to my theatricals.

To be honest, her reaction left a lot to be desired. Instead of gnashing her teeth and raging around the room in frustration at her scheme being thwarted, she sat at her desk looking at me as if I was a particularly interesting specimen of insect. The feeling that she knew something I didn't grew stronger.

'Tuffets, eh? Now that's a bit of a nuisance and no mistake,' she said. 'What specific tuffet are you talking about?'

'The tuffet in the back garden of the B&B; the one that Miss Muffet's family have been sitting on to eat their curds and whey for generations. Surely you've heard the song 'Little Miss Muffet sat on a tuffet...' and so on. Tuffets are considered to be of immense historic importance, so they cannot be dug up, built over or altered in any way. It was in the paper. So even if you get the building, you still won't be able to build your road through it. Or if you do, I suspect you'll be neck deep in lawyers, archaeologists, environmentalists and politicians, all of whom will tie you up in enough red-tape to stall the building work for years.'

Edna grinned – the 'I have you now and you're not going to like it' grin. She slumped back into her chair and pressed a button on the desk. Seconds later a well-dressed and superior-looking gentleman entered the room carrying a folder. He had bureaucrat written all over him. 'You rang, ma'am,' he said, nose in the air.

'Tuffets, Laurence. They are protected, aren't they?'

'Yes, ma'am,' he replied. He was very well spoken.

'And that includes the tuffet in the Curds and Whey B&B?'

'Why, yes, ma'am.'

'The tuffet that we investigated when we were planning the motorway?'

'Why, yes again, ma'am.' He seemed to be enjoying this almost as much as Edna. I could sense she was about to spring her surprise and I knew it wouldn't be pleasant.

'The self-same tuffet that we agreed not to disturb and altered our plans so the motorway would go over and not through the premises?'

'Ma'am, you are, of course, correct once more.' And he looked at me and smirked.

Over the B&B?

Not through? Over?

Edna slapped the desktop and howled with glee. It was as if she could read my thoughts – which probably wasn't all that difficult as the expression on my face gave them away.

'Yes, Harry, over the B&B. So you see, we didn't need to put Miss Muffet out of business at all. In fact, she was never going to interfere with our plans. I do believe you've had a wasted journey – at least from your perspective. From my point of view, I don't think it's been wasted at all. In fact, I've quite enjoyed our little tête-à-tête. It certainly makes up for the last time we met.'

I didn't doubt it. Our last encounter resulted in her losing out on a very valuable antique and having a spell placed on her bodyguards. It was payback time.

Happy that he'd been both of service to his mistress and had helped in the humiliation of one of her most hated foes, Laurence slimed out of the room, leaving me to face a gloating Edna.

'So you see, Pigg, you were wrong. Wrong, wrong, wrong. Just wait until word gets out, and, trust me, word will get out.' She was taking great pleasure in my discomfiture.

I decided that a dignified withdrawal was in order. Gesturing to Miss Muffet to follow, I stuck my snout in the air and strode purposefully out the door of Edna's office, her raucous laughter, the howling of orcs and roars of her gorillas all echoing around my humiliated head as I left.

I wasn't let be humiliated for long. We were no sooner out the door when Miss Muffet turned on me. She was, understandably, a bit miffed that things hadn't gone entirely to plan and, despite my (now battered) confidence, we were no further down the road to solving the case.

'Please, Miss Muffet,' I said in my most soothing and placatory voice (it was something I was actually good at – I regularly had to placate disgruntled clients). 'This was only the first step in solving the case. At least we've eliminated Edna and her construction company from our enquiries. Prior to this she was our main suspect.'

'Our only suspect,' Miss Muffet pointed out, somewhat miffed.

'Our only suspect for now,' I replied. 'Trust me; by the end of the day, I expect we'll have loads more.'

I didn't realise at the time exactly how prophetic that comment was going to be.

5

Jack Has a Bright Idea

I was back in the office once more. I seemed to be spending an awful lot of time there, which was probably a good indication that the case wasn't going too well. All my leads had turned out to be useless and – reluctant though I was to admit it – I was stumped. This case seemed to have more red herrings than a communist fishmonger and, to add insult to injury, even Edna had got one-up on me. Now, as if to mock my incompetence, I was depending on my two 'partners' for assistance – and that was something I never thought I'd hear myself say.

To be fair, both of them were taking the case seriously and were coming up with ideas, even if most of them were either useless or wildly impractical.

'That is most strange,' Basili mused when I told them about my visit to Frogg Prince Pets. 'I would have been most certain that a vile orc person would have been belonging to Edna.'

Another vile person, I thought. 'Well, if what she said is true then she is really out of the equation and I've no reason to doubt her. Her story is too easy to check out. And if he's not Edna's then whose is he? I thought she had the market cornered in cheap orc labour.'

'The orc is one thing, but if it's not Edna and it's not that mad old woman who lives in the Shoe Hotel, then who's doing it?' said Jack.

'That's the question, isn't it,' I replied. 'If we knew that, then we wouldn't be here, would we?'

Then Basili asked the question that set the wheels spinning – or at least rotating slowly – in my mind once more.

'Why are all those people still staying in this place?'

I know the same question had crossed my mind when I visited Miss Muffet's earlier, but I hadn't given it much thought since. Basili did have a point.

'I don't know, but it would want to be a very good reason, wouldn't it?'

'Indeed, many people are being most scared of spiders and they certainly would not be staying anywhere where creatures like that are in such large numbers.'

'If I was them, I'd have moved out ages ago,' said Jack. 'I don't mind creepy-crawlies, but it can't be a lot of fun staying there with webs and stuff.'

'That's why I intend to go back there and talk to them. If they have a reason then I need to know what it is. Maybe then I can get some idea of who's responsible for the spiders.'

'Oh, yes, once more we are doing the interviews,' exclaimed Basili, clapping his hands in excitement. 'I love when we are talking to our suspects.'

Jack raised his hand. 'But won't that sort of give the game away. If they know we're investigators, won't they just lie to us? We won't find anything out that way.'

'You know Jack, you're right. There must be another way, one that won't make it obvious who we are.'

Jack's hand was still in the air. 'I've got a great idea, Harry.'

I doubted it, but I indicated for him to continue.

'Remember when we were at the North Pole and we needed to get information from that bogus elf?'

I nodded. 'Why is that relevant?'

'Disguises.'

'Excuse me?'

'We could disguise ourselves as guests.' Jack waved his arms in excitement. 'No one would know who we are and we could mingle, talk to everyone and make them reveal something.'

I was about to point out how difficult it would be to disguise a pig, a fat ex-genie and a small boy as anything that would successfully pass muster when Basili chimed in.

'Oh, that is a most excellent idea, young Jack. We are going undercover in a secret mission. How exciting.'

And how stupid, I thought. We'd never get away with it. We wouldn't last ten minutes in the B&B. But the more I thought about it, the more the idea refused to go away. Maybe it could work. Our cover would have to be spectacular if we were to avoid discovery, but it might be the only way to find out what was going on. At least that was my justification when I agreed to it. In fact, I was so desperate and unable to come up with any other idea that, really, I had no choice.

'Okay then, we're going undercover.' I said.

Jack jumped up and down in excitement.

'But not you,' I said to him. 'It could be dangerous.'

'Yes, but you didn't say that when I was disguised as the elf, did you?' His disappointment was obvious.

'But this is much more dangerous. We won't be able to keep our eye on you like we did then and there's always the danger of blowing your cover.'

'May I be making a suggestion,' Basili interrupted.

I waved at him to continue.

'Mr Harry and I will be talking to the guests, yes?'

I nodded.

'Well, will we not be needing a someone to be keeping an eye on the people who are working there too?'

'Yes,' Jack shouted. 'I could be in the kitchen, helping out and stuff and, at the same time, keeping my eyes open.'

It made sense and he'd probably be safe enough there. After all, what harm could come to him in a kitchen?

'All right then team, it's agreed. Now what shall we go as?'

6

A Bit of a Drag

'**A**re you guys really serious about this?' Gloria, my receptionist, had offered to give some tips on make-up and clothes, but seemed to be having second thoughts now that she'd actually seen our disguises. At that moment she was touching up my face with mascara and gloss – whatever they were – and seemed to be finding it tremendously difficult to refrain from smirking – if not guffawing loudly. 'There,' she said, putting her magical make-up kit away. 'You're done, but I have to say it: even if you put lipstick on a pig, it's still a pig.'

With as much dignity as I could muster – which wasn't a lot considering I was wearing a long blonde wig, high heels and a black minidress – I pointed out that, as ideas went, our one had legs (and probably better ones than mine) and, if it came off (insert whatever gratuitous pun you like here), would probably help hugely in breaking the case.

I stood up and tottered around the office, teetering from side to side as I tried to keep my balance. 'How do women stay upright in these heels,' I asked. 'Is tightrope walking a genetic trait that all women have, or something?'

'You'll get used to it eventually, though I'm not sure you'll be ready by the time you go undercover.' Gloria paused for a second and looked even more closely at me. 'Remind me again, who are you supposed to be exactly and, more to the point, why are you going in that ridiculous outfit?'

'I am Harriet du Crêpe and I am the personal assistant and general dogsbody for that well-known foreign movie-director Alain Schmidt-Heye, and I'm dressed like this as there's a distinct possibility someone may have noticed me earlier when I visited the B&B and I don't want to be recognised. If they know I'm a detective then the game will be up.'

Gloria began to erupt into gales of laughter. 'So let me get this right. You, a large male pig, are going undercover as a female PA to an international movie-director who can only be—' She never got to finish her sentence. Before she could say any more, the door from my office, where Basili had been changing, opened and he entered the room. His entrance certainly had an impact, although not, perhaps, the one we might have expected. Gloria collapsed on the desk, laughing uncontrollably, tears of hilarity streaming from her eyes.

'Is your lady assistant being most amused at my outfit?' said a somewhat indignant Basili. 'I am thinking that, after studying pictures of many famous directors of movies, that it is perhaps a most accurate representation.'

I wasn't sure what illustrations he'd actually studied, but I wasn't convinced that his outfit was as representative as he thought. Brown knee-high riding boots covered tan plus-fours. On his upper body, a lurid red smoking jacket and a white silk shirt jostled for prominence. The overall over-the-top effect was completed by a white silk scarf draped casually around his neck, white gloves, a cigarette holder (with no actual cigarette) dangling from his mouth and a black beret rakishly plonked on his head. He did look a bit extreme, but time wasn't on our side. We had to make do with what we were able to pick up at Freddie's Fancy Dress Store, having sent Basili out with a shopping list.

In hindsight, maybe I should have gone myself. But it was too late now.

Gloria had recovered some of her composure. 'So you go into Miss Muffet's B&B, you snoop around dressed like that and you hope people are going to give something away – other than an award for the most ludicrous outfit in the house. And on that note, how exactly are you going to justify your presence there in the first instance?'

'Our story is that we're scouting locations for a haunted house movie that Basili – I mean Mr Schmidt-Heye – will be filming early next year. Miss Muffet's is a prime candidate, I think you'll agree.'

'I'll take your word for it, but I think you need to get in character, Harry; the voice needs to be a little higher, otherwise people will see through your disguise – assuming they don't cop to you as soon as you walk in the door.'

I puffed out my (enhanced) chest indignantly. 'I was a very talented actor when I was younger, I'll have you know. I played a leading role in my school's Nativity play and my performance got great reviews in the school newsletter.'

Gloria looked like she was biting her lip. 'If you say so,' she said. 'On a more serious note, how are you going to get to Miss Muffet's? You're going to have to look the part from the moment you arrive.'

'Hah, I knew you'd ask that. Ali Baba still owes me a favour after I sorted him out at Christmas, so he's allowing me to use one of his stretch magic carpets. It'll make quite an entrance.'

'Could you not have used an ordinary limo; you know, one with actual wheels?'

'I couldn't afford to rent one and, anyway, Ali doesn't use them; he flies everywhere, so magic carpet it is.'

'Just as long as you don't fall off,' smirked Gloria.

'This isn't one of the sporty, streamlined ones Ali normally uses. It's a big one with loads of room – and seat-belts. We should be fine. Anyway, it's a short ride when you're not on the ground.'

I gestured to Basili. 'Right Mr Director, you ready to go?'

'But Mr Harry, I know nothing about the making of the movies. What will I be saying if someone should be talking to me?'

'Look, you're a big-time movie-director so act like one. You haven't got time to speak to mere mortals like the guests at the B&B. If anyone tries to engage you in conversation, just sneer and refer them to me. As your PA, my job is to answer any questions. While we're in there, your job is to listen, okay? Just think of these words and you'll be fine: arrogant, superior, enigmatic.'

Basili nodded. 'Ah, now I am seeing. You want me to be acting just like you.'

Before I could reply with furious indignation at the slur on my impeccable character, the phone on Gloria's desk rang. 'Yes,' she said, 'they're here. I'll send them right out.' Hanging up, she said, 'Your magic carpet awaits.'

Together, Basili and I headed for the door.

'Be careful, won't you?' Gloria said, grinning. 'And remember: stay in character at all times, you don't want to blow your cover.'

'We'll be fine, daaaaarling,' I drawled in my finest PA voice.

I could have sworn I heard an 'I'm not so sure' from the office as the door closed behind us, but I couldn't be certain.

I was so eager to get to Miss Muffet's and begin our undercover operation that I made a fatal mistake as I closed the door behind me. I still hadn't quite mastered the art of woman, walking so, forgetting to take off my shoes, I teetered on the landing and took a tentative step forward before stumbling over the first step and sliding down the rest of them on my backside, landing in an undignified heap on the floor below. There are twenty-four steps from my office to street level and I felt every single one of them as I bounced my way down.

Struggling to my feet, I tugged my dress down and, ignoring the smirks of our chauffeur, clambered aboard the stretch magic carpet, making sure I was securely strapped in before taking off. On our way across town, I briefed Basili some more on the dos and don'ts of being a movie-director.

'When we get there, do not get off this carpet until I say so. It's my job to make sure that everything is ready for you inside. Say nothing unless I ask you a question and nod knowingly if I point anything out. Do not open any doors; I'll make sure they are opened for you. You will eat alone at a separate table. That will give you an opportunity to study everyone as I'll be eating with them.'

Basili looked uncertain. 'I am not so sure about this. What if I am making a mistake?'

'Don't worry about it, I'll be there to clean up any mess, but, if you don't say anything, there's probably no way you'll get into trouble.' Considering his track record I wasn't so sure, but I had to build up his confidence as best I could.

The Curds and Whey Mystery

The fresh air blasting our faces as we threaded our way through the buildings of downtown Grimmtown reminded me of something that, despite its obviousness, I had completely failed to take into consideration: the ex-genie's flatulence problem. 'Basili, under no circumstances are you to fart. It will completely undermine your credibility. I might be able to argue one or two of them away as sewage problems or something, but if it happens consistently it may damage our relationship with the guests.' Not to mention their lungs, vision and general well-being.

'I will do my utmost, Mr Harry, but it is a most remarkably difficult thing to do.'

As if I didn't have enough problems already.

'Where is Jack?' asked Basili. 'Surely he is being here with us?'

'He's already at the B&B, settling in. I spoke to his mother and got her okay for him to be a kitchen boy at weekends. Not only will he let us know what's going on behind the scenes with the staff, but he'll get a bit of pocket money as well. The only drawback is he'll have to work for it.'

'Ah, yes, of course, the staff. Isn't it always the butler that is doing these things? Perhaps we should be taking a closer look at this man.'

'No, Basili, it isn't, and I'm not even sure Miss Muffet employs a butler. Let's not start jumping to conclusions just yet.'

51

'You are right.' His face dropped. 'I am still so very new to this game of detectives. I have very much to learn.'

I patted him on the shoulder. 'But you're learning all the time. We're nearly there, so remember what I told you and, above all, please don't fart.'

Basili gave me a weak and totally unconvincing smile as the magic carpet glided to a halt outside the B&B.

'Okay, we're on. Don't move until I get back. If anyone tries to engage you in conversation just ignore them and act superior.'

Basili nodded and looked glum.

I rummaged in my handbag. 'Here, wear these,' I said, handing him a pair of sunglasses. He looked at them doubtfully.

'But we are in winter and there is no sun to be shining.'

'It doesn't matter. Movie people wear shades all the time, indoors and outdoors. It's a sort of a trademark.' And it will hide some more of your face, I said to myself.

Right, it was time to get fully into character. Chest out, balance, do not wobble and remember you're a PA. I recited this little mantra over and over as I hopped gingerly down from the magic carpet. Taking a deep breath, I stepped forward, put my shoe down very carefully and then repeated the operation with my other foot. I found that if I swayed gently from side to side it made walking a little bit easier. Balancing like I was on the deck of a small ship in a hurricane, I rolled towards the door of the B&B, opened it and stepped into the world of the movie business.

7

Quiet on Set

What did I know about being a PA? Very little. The sum total of my research had been three gossip magazines Gloria kept in her desk drawer and a quick viewing of a documentary on the Grimmtown Film Festival. It didn't make me an expert, but it gave me something to go on as I entered Miss Muffet's B&B.

'No, no, no, this won't do at all,' I shrieked as I strode purposefully into the lobby. 'Mr Schmidt-Heye must have total privacy. This area must be cleared at once.'

As there was no one there apart from Miss Muffet herself, who was manning the reception desk, it probably didn't have the effect I was expecting, but I figured I might as well get into character immediately.

'Mr Pigg, is that you?' Miss Muffet seemed to have difficulty deciding whether to laugh or to stare. Maybe I should have briefed her in a bit more detail about our plans.

'Yes,' I hissed. 'But today I'm Harriet du Crêpe, remember?'

'I know, you told me. I just wasn't expecting...this,' she whispered back.

I didn't ask her to elaborate; I just requested that she play along.

By now, some of the guests, attracted no doubt by my high-decibel delivery, were gathering on the first-floor landing and at the entrance to the dining room.

'Please,' I shouted. 'Can we have everyone out of here now?'

'What's going on?' asked a small, old man at the dining-room door. 'Is there a fire? Should we evacuate? I'll get my coat.'

'No, no.' Miss Muffet tried to defuse the situation. 'We have a new guest arriving and he likes his privacy. Perhaps if you could all go back to what you were doing, we might get it sorted out.'

'So there's no fire then?'

'No.'

'Or any emergency?'

'Definitely not.'

'Good,' said the old man. 'I'm going back to my breakfast then.'

'Thank you, Mr Spratt,' Miss Muffet said. 'Coffee should be along shortly. That's Jack Spratt,' she whispered to me as the guests began to disperse. 'He's here with his wife. They stayed here after they got married and are revisiting now to celebrate their anniversary.'

From the look of him, that would have been about two hundred years ago. 'And they're still staying here despite the...um...difficulties.'

'Oh, yes, they're quite adamant. Apparently it has huge nostalgic value for them.'

It would want to, I thought. It's the only reason anyone would want to stay here.

Figuring that Basili had been waiting outside long enough, I decided it was time for his grand entrance. 'Good,' I announced. 'The area is clear. Mr Schmidt-Heye can enter now.' I rushed outside and beckoned at the chauffeur.

'What?' he grunted.

'Help Mr Schmidt-Heye down.'

'Hey, Ali Baba said I was only to drive you here. He said nothing about this.'

The prospect of helping a large ex-genie off a magic carpet while wearing heels didn't appeal to me. 'Just do it, okay. Do you really want me to tell him you wouldn't help us?'

With a resigned groan, he got off the carpet, walked around to the side and held out his arm. 'Okay, big guy, down you get.'

'Respect, please,' I ordered. 'This is a famous movie-director. You will refer to him as "sir" at all times.'

'No, he's not. He's that fat bloke that hangs around with you when you're not wearing a dress. He's a movie-director in the same way that I'm an astronaut.'

'Keep your voice down, you'll blow our cover.'

The chauffeur smirked. 'Oh, I think you're doing that all by yourself. You don't need my help.'

I marched up to him and grabbed him in a very unlady-like way. 'Just oblige me, okay?'

The chauffeur's face turned white as I tightened my grip. 'You're the boss,' he wheezed and turned to Basili. 'If...sir... would care to take my arm.'

'That's much better,' I said as he helped Basili down from the magic carpet. 'I'll see your boss gets a good report.'

The chauffeur glowered as he jumped back into his seat, but, sensibly, refused to comment any further. Seconds later the magic carpet shot into the sky and we were on our own once more.

'Right, we're good to go. I've cleared the reception area, so, hopefully, no one will approach us. Remember, if they do, let me do the talking.'

Basili nodded glumly and followed me inside where Miss Muffet was waiting to greet her newest guest. 'Mr Schmidt-Heye, what a great honour it is having you here in our humble abode.' Wow, she certainly knew how to fawn. Then I noticed that she was looking at Basili expectantly. I nudged him hard in the ribs. 'That's you, remember?'

'Yes, you are most welcome.' He tapped his cigarette holder on the edge of the reception desk. 'Now please to be showing me my room. I must lie down. It has been a most horrendous trip.'

Wow, the ride from my office hadn't been that bad.

'Yes, of course. Your room is this way. If you'll follow me.' Miss Muffet led us up the stairs. Lining the wall all the way up was a series of paintings. I glanced at them as we passed. They all seemed to show pictures of the same person doing something adventurous. In one picture he was waving to a large group of people on the ground as he ascended in a hot-air balloon; in another he was in a speedboat waving once more at a pursuing fleet.

'Family portraits?' I asked Miss Muffet.

'Sort of,' she replied, but made no attempt to elaborate further.

I shrugged my shoulders, but decided to drop the subject, seeing as she clearly didn't want to talk about it. But something about the pictures nagged at me. For some reason, the person featured in them rang a bell, but recognition just wouldn't come.

We arrived on the first-floor landing and were led into a large bedroom at the front of the house. To her credit, Miss Muffet had made a huge effort to remove any trace of spiders, but they were already reclaiming the corners and would probably have retaken the whole room by teatime.

Basili looked around, his head in the air. 'I am supposing this will have to do,' he sniffed, running a gloved finger along the dressing table and holding it up for scrutiny.

'It's okay, Basili,' I whispered. 'We're on our own now. No one can see you. You can drop the act.'

'Thank goodness for that,' he said as he collapsed on the bed, which groaned ominously at the intrusion. 'Being an undercover operative is being most difficult.'

'You've only been undercover for five minutes and all you've had to do is walk up a flight of stairs, how difficult can it be?'

'Ah, yes, but I am struggling greatly to find my inner director and my motivation. Why am I doing this? What are this man's issues and struggles?'

He seemed to be taking his acting a bit too seriously. 'Look, you're not auditioning for a role in a real film. Just stand around and be superior like we said. Just stay shtum and you'll be fine.'

We were interrupted by a knock on the door. 'Quick, back in character,' I ordered. 'Who is it? Mr Schmidt-Heye is resting after his long journey and cannot be disturbed.'

'Harry, it's me, Jack,' whispered a voice from outside the door. I quickly opened it and dragged Jack into the room. He took one look at us and fell on the floor laughing.

'Jack, this isn't the time,' I said. 'What have you to report?'

With difficulty, Jack composed himself and sat up. 'I'm working in the kitchen, but it's not a very nice place.

The cook, Mrs Hubbard, is very bossy. I don't think she likes me.'

Miss Muffet nodded at Jack's comment. 'Mrs Hubbard runs a tight kitchen. Just do as she says, work hard and you'll be okay.'

'And then there's the waiter or butler or whatever he is. He's a bit strange; won't talk to anyone.'

'Aha,' said Basili. 'I am being right, there is a butler. He is doing the crime.'

'Oh, don't be ridiculous, old Mr Zingiber has been with the family for years. He looks after serving the meals and making sure the guests are being cared for. He's certainly not responsible for this crime.'

Jack pulled at the hem of my dress. 'And I think he's made of gingerbread too. I'm terrified in case I spill something on him and he melts.'

Miss Muffet overheard. 'Don't worry about him; he's pretty stale by now. It'd take quite a deluge to soften him up.'

'Anyone else in the kitchen I should know about?' I asked.

'Just Polly. She helps Mrs Hubbard with the cooking. She's a nice girl; none too bright, but very good with food, making tea, that sort of thing,' said Miss Muffet.

It was time to bring the meeting to order. 'Right, now that everyone's here, let's go over it once more: look out for anyone acting suspiciously, don't talk to anyone unless you have to and, if you find anything out, come and tell me.

Got that?' Nods all around. 'Good, now let's go and solve this case.'

Jack scurried back to the kitchen and Miss Muffet made to follow him. She turned to me as she reached the door. 'Will you be dining with us tonight?'

The thought of hundreds of spiders watching me as I ate, waiting for an opportunity to help themselves, made my stomach cartwheel, but I had to meet the other guests. 'Mr Schmidt-Heye will dine at a table alone; I will eat with the other guests.'

'Very good. Dinner is at seven.'

Yeah: me, the guests and a tribe of tarantulas. 'Lovely,' I muttered. 'Oh, by the way, where's my room?'

'I put you in the room next door. Unfortunately, we didn't have time to clean it out. I'm afraid you'll just have to ignore the spiders.'

Fantastic.

8

A Bluffer's Guide to Polite Conversation

The dining room looked like it had been decorated for a wedding. White strands of web hung in all the corners and were draped like netting across the furniture. Miss Havisham would have felt right at home here. Someone had made an effort to clean the room; the webs on the floor had been swept into corners where they piled up like indoor snowdrifts. As it was evening the spiders were more active too. Armies of them marched across the floor or dangled from the ceiling seeking out food. Miss Muffet had thought ahead though. As well as kitchen-boy duties, Jack had been drafted in, with a sweeping brush, to attack any arachnids that came too close.

He was being kept very busy.

In order to maintain appearances as well as giving Basili an opportunity to eavesdrop, I'd managed to get him a table all to himself in the corner, where he was the subject of many curious looks. If anyone tried to approach the table I intercepted them with a 'Mr Schmidt-Heye wants to be alone' and what I thought was a very forbidding stare. It seemed to work, as any would-be fans slunk away without disturbing him.

Satisfied that Basili wouldn't be talking to anyone, I left him to his meal and took my seat at the nearest table. Mr Spratt and a woman I assumed to be Mrs Spratt sat on either side of me. Across the table was a pompous-looking gentleman. 'Nimble. John B. Nimble,' he'd replied curtly when I'd introduced myself. 'Antiques.' I wasn't sure whether he was referring to his job or to the other two guests at the table. Then he went back to reading his newspaper, ignoring the rest of us.

'Charming,' I muttered.

'Oh, he's not too bad once you get to know him,' said Mr Spratt. 'By the way, I'm Jack and this is my wife, Muriel.' He indicated his wife, who was as round as he was thin, and she gave me a tiny wave. Side by side they looked like the number 10 and were in direct contrast to John Nimble in that they never stopped talking. Muriel Spratt had confirmed what Miss Muffet had said: the Spratts were celebrating fifty years of marriage by returning to the guest house they'd stayed in for their honeymoon. Miss Muffet's B&B in Grimmtown; wow, they had really pushed the boat out the day they got married.

'And how about you dear?' asked Mrs Spratt. 'Is there any romance in your life?'

'I'm firmly focused on my career,' I bluffed. 'There's no time in my life for a relationship at present', which wasn't entirely untrue either.

As I watched I couldn't help but notice that the Spratts had a strange habit of sharing the contents of their plates with each other. She'd cut the fat off her meat and pass the rest on to her husband and he reciprocated by passing the fat from his food on to her plate. They ate so fast they got to finish everything before the spiders got to it. Mrs Spratt noticed me watching them eat and giggled nervously. 'It's a diet thing,' she said. 'He likes the lean bits and I like the rest, so we never go hungry.'

I spent the rest of the meal beating spiders away from my plate as I tried to eat my salad faster than they could steal it. It was a close contest, but victory was mine – the dead arachnids scattered around my plate testament to the brutal struggle. All the way through I fielded questions about Basili's solitude; all my answers being variations on a theme of being anti-social with a fear of being touched or spoken to.

After dinner we all migrated to the lounge for 'mingling and conversation', as Miss Muffet put it. From what I could see, it seemed to mean an evening of awkward silences and everyone standing around looking very self-conscious. In fact, until one of the guests, Mr Nocchio, a tall, thin gentleman with a funny lumbering gait and skin the texture of wood, came up and quizzed me about Basili, who was standing behind me still trying to look superior, we might have all been in a very arty silent movie (in black and white, of course).

'Who eez thees movie-director you 'ave behind you?' he asked in heavily accented English.

'He's the famous Alain Schmidt-Heye,' I replied haughtily.

'Famous? I 'ave not 'eard of 'eem.'

There was a chorus of 'me neither's as everyone in the room suddenly took an interest in our conversation. It was time for some arty-type bluffing.

'Of course you haven't heard of him, unless you're the kind of discerning movie-goer who enjoys documentaries. He's very highly thought of on the global cinematic stage.' Attacking their artistic pretensions while fabricating Basili's cinematic catalogue might divert their interest. If they figured they didn't know as much about high art as they thought, they might just go along with what I was saying so as not to appear less cultured. Ah, intellectual snobbery, how I admire thee.

'Ah, yes, now that you mention it, I do recall reading something about him in the arts section of the *Grimmtown Globe*. Didn't he do that film on the secret life of Prince Charming?' said a well-dressed man leaning against the mantelpiece at the far side of the room. I was surprised he'd even noticed us; he seemed to be constantly keeping Miss Muffet in his eye line as she hovered around her guests, making sure they were comfortable. What was making her so interesting, I wondered? This well-dressed man now needed to be kept in my eye line; that was suspicious behaviour – in my book at any rate.

'Yes, that was one of Mr Schmidt-Heye's,' I replied, going with the flow. 'It was very well received and there are rumours it may get nominated for a Gifty.' If I was going to bluff, I might as well go all the way and spin out as convincing a back-story as I could. It would only have to hold up to scrutiny for another day or so. After that it hopefully wouldn't matter.

'Gifty? What's a Gifty?' asked a small, dapper man, sitting in one of the armchairs by the fire.

'It's the Grimmtown International Film and Television Awards, darling,' I said, rolling my eyes. 'Goodness, do you people know anything about culture?'

There was a brief pause followed by much knowing nodding and variations on 'Ah, the Awards. I didn't realise they were known as Giftys by the masses.' Nothing like intellectual pretension to aid in a cover-up.

Basili nodded smugly and raised his cigarette holder to his mouth once more.

The dapper man, whom, based on a process of elimination, I suspected to be either Thomas Piper or William Winkie, stood up and walked across the room towards me.

Uh, oh, I thought. This isn't good.

'I much preferred your earlier, funnier material,' he said, trying to approach Basili. 'Don't you do that kind of stuff any more?'

I interrupted and blocked the spoofer. 'Mr Schmidt-Heye appreciates his fans, but doesn't like to be touched. You may address any comments through me.'

Then, to my horror, Basili decided to engage in some role-play – and in direct contravention of orders. 'There is a favourite film of mine that you are liking? I am most gratified to meet a true fan, and, perhaps, you are telling us your name.' Nice one Basili; maybe he might turn out to be good at this after all.

The dapper man preened at being acknowledged. 'Willie Winkie's the name,' he said, stretching out a hand that I immediately slapped away, giving him a warning look at the same time.

If he was Winkie then the man by the fireplace must be Thomas Piper. Licken and Lurkey I already knew – and, fortunately, they weren't in the room – so that meant that the only person I hadn't met was Queenie Harte.

So far, so good – now all I had to do was find out what they did. 'Mr Schmidt-Heye is thinking about moving from documentaries into dramatic motion pictures. To that end he is engaging with a number of significant backers with a view to raising funds for this exciting venture. If any of you are interested, perhaps you might provide me with your details. So far, all our investors have received a significant return on their investment.'

There was an excited murmuring and a swathe of business cards was thrust into my trotters.

'What kind of movie are you considering making?' The formerly abrupt Mr Nimble sat up straight in his chair and suddenly seemed very interested too.

'We've received a very promising script for a horror film that we believe we can use to take the genre into significantly new directions. In fact, that's why we're staying here. We feel that it may be a great location for some of the opening scenes, set in a haunted house.' More nodding and knowing looks – suddenly they were all experts.

Ah, what a bit of pandering to artistic snobbery can get you.

Just as they were all falling over themselves to tell me how great Basili was, how they were secretly fans of his all along and how they'd be most interested in discussing investment opportunities, there was the sound of the front door banging and loud shouting from the hallway. Every head – except mine and Piper's – swivelled apprehensively towards the lounge door. I turned to Basili and whispered, 'Be on your toes, things might get a bit out of hand.'

He looked confused. 'Why, Mr Harry, what is happening?'

Before I could answer, the lounge door crashed open and in walked a giant chicken garbed in a clown costume, followed closely by a much smaller turkey dressed as a nun. My worst fears were confirmed: Licken and Lurkey had come home to roost – and from the way his eyes narrowed, Licken had immediately seen through my disguise. It was time for some quick action. I rushed towards him arms outstretched. 'Licken darling, it's been so long. How ARE you?' I exclaimed while grabbing him by the shoulders and attempting an air-kiss. *Mwuah, Mwuah.* 'Don't let on it's me,' I whispered into his ear. 'I'll explain later. As far as you're concerned I'm Harriet, okay?'

To his credit, Licken bought into my story and nodded vacantly, trying to catch up with what was going on.

'And Lurkey too, how wonderful!' Another air-kiss, followed up with a hug that squeezed the breath out of him before he could say anything. 'Not a word,' I hissed. 'Or I tell all about you know what.'

Before he could respond, I turned to the other guests. 'I'm sure you've all already met Grimmtown's foremost comedy duo, Lurkey and Licken,' I announced. 'They're very old and very dear friends of mine,' a statement that wasn't exactly untrue either. 'They're such darling people and I'm so glad to see them again after such a long time.' Behind me I could hear Lurkey gasping for air while Licken seemed to be whispering in his ear. Hopefully Lurkey wouldn't say anything stupid, though he was by far the dumber of that particular duo, so I wasn't sure he'd caught on. Licken, on the other hand, was giving it large.

The Curds and Whey Mystery

'Ah, yes, our dear friend Harriet. Remember when she used to sell ice-cream at the Grimmtown Grand Old Comedy and then the punters used to chuck it right back at her. Ah, she's come a long way since then.' Then he caught sight of Basili. 'Is that who I think it is? Surely it can't be—'

'Yes, you're right,' I interrupted before he said something stupid. 'It's Alain Schmidt-Heye,' adding, 'the famous movie-director', when I saw the confused look on his face.

'Oh, yeah, right; him,' Licken stammered, clearly confused.

I needed to get them out of the room before they gave something away, but at the same time I couldn't leave Basili there on his own with his new fan club. He'd definitely give something away.

'Sir,' – I grabbed Basili by the arm – 'perhaps we could take these two fine gentlemen outside to catch up, so as not to bore our other friends here.'

'Nonsense,' said Willie Winkie. 'We wouldn't be bored at all. I'm sure your tales of the glamorous showbiz life you lead would be the perfect after-dinner conversation piece.'

I was about to spin out an excuse as to why we had to leave the room right that second – just as soon as I could think of one – when I saw something that sent the case in an entirely new and unwelcome direction. Above the mantelpiece, almost totally obscured by webs, was a portrait. This wasn't just any portrait, though. Oh, no, even hidden by all those strands of webbing, the face in the picture was immediately

71

recognisable: Grimmtown's most notorious pirate, Sinbad El Muhfte. Now that I could see his face clearly, I also recognised him as the subject in all those pictures on the stairway wall.

Then the links began to coalesce in my mind.

El Muhfte. Not much of a stretch to Muffet.

Sinbad El Muhfte and Miss Muffet; the names were slightly different, but the similarity was surely no coincidence.

Now, looking more closely at the portrait, I could see the family resemblance and the awful truth struck me: Miss Muffet must be Sinbad's daughter. The daughter of one of the most famous criminals in the town's history, who was currently doing a twenty-to-life stretch in Grimmtown's maximum security prison. And in all the pictures on the stairway wall, he wasn't waving to adoring fans, as I had originally assumed; oh no, they were portraits of him taunting the pursuing police, having successfully evaded them once more.

Now I'm not a great believer in coincidences, so considering who daddy was and combining it with Miss Muffet's current predicament, I got a horrible feeling that this case had just taken a major turn for the worse – and I was smack in the middle of it.

9

*At Midnight,
All the Detectives*

I tried not to show any reaction, but Basili sensed something was wrong. 'Ms du Crêpe,' he whispered. 'You are fine, yes?'

I waved him away. 'Yes, yes, I'm okay. I'm just a bit faint. Must have been something I ate.'

Willie Winkie grabbed me by the elbow and escorted me to one of the fireside armchairs. 'Here, sit down.' He turned to the other guests. 'Can someone get a glass of water?'

I tried to stand up, but a restraining arm kept me firmly in the seat. 'I'm fine, honestly.' It was time for some drama. I slumped across the chair and brought my hand to my forehead. 'I'm just feeling a little light-headed; perhaps if someone can help me to my room, some rest might do me good.'

A glass of liquid was thrust into my trotters. 'Here, drink this,' said Willie Winkie.

I grabbed the glass and emptied it in a single slug – and promptly nearly brought it back up again when the burning liquid hit my stomach. It felt like I was dying. My lungs heaved for breath and my eyes were streaming tears. Had someone seen through my cover and tried to poison me?

'Nothing like a glass of brandy to sort you out,' bellowed John Nimble. 'I always have a snifter after my evening meal. Good for the internal workings.'

So, not poison then. Based on what I'd drunk, I figured my internal workings would never work the same again. I waved my arms at Basili and between coughs and noisy intakes of air I managed to wheeze the word 'bed'. Basili took the hint, dragged me to my feet and hauled me out of the lounge. It wasn't the most dignified of exits, but at least it worked. Supporting me on his shoulder, he struggled manfully upstairs before dropping me on the floor of his room. I hit the ground with an undignified thud.

'Sorry, Mr Harry,' he apologised. 'I am not being able to carry you any further.'

I lay on the carpet gasping. 'Now I really do need a glass of water.' I was gasping even more when one was flung in my face. 'Please be snapping out of it,' said Basili. 'It was only a glass of brandy. Now perhaps you are explaining the meaning of your behaviour.'

Dripping, I hauled myself upright and managed to stagger to the bed. Sitting on the edge I faced the ex-genie, took a deep breath and tried to explain what I'd seen.

The Curds and Whey Mystery

'Sinbad El Muhfte, pirate, freebooter and all round bad guy is Miss Muffet's father,' I said, a tad dramatically. The effect was lessened by the blank expression on Basili's face. 'You've never heard of Sinbad?'

Basili shook his head doubtfully. 'I knew of a Sinbad many years ago when I was very young. He was an adventurer and having the most exciting time. Is it being the same person?'

'Your Sinbad was this Sinbad's ancestor, if memory serves. Sinbad El Muhfte was Grimmtown's most notorious pirate. Basically, he helped himself to the contents of any ship that tried to sail into the port. It impacted the sea-trade in and out of the city for years until he was finally captured and jailed for a very long time.'

'So?' asked Basili.

'So, the big question that people asked after he was sent down was: what happened to all his riches? He had looted lots of valuable antiques, paintings, that sort of thing. He was quite the collector. From what I remember, he didn't put it in banks or invest too much of it so as to keep the law off his trail. There were lots of rumours that he'd hidden it somewhere. Over the years people have tried to find where he'd stashed it, but eventually, when no one found anything, they began to believe that it never existed. The rumours eventually died out.'

'But why is that having anything to be doing with our present case?' asked Basili.

'It may not, but if someone got wind of where the fortune was stashed and let's just say that it was somewhere in this house – which was probably his house after all – then wouldn't it be very easy to search if the owner had been scared off the premises?'

'Is it not being stretching things just a little bit?' said Basili. 'I am still thinking that someone trying to be putting Miss Muffet out of business is a most strong motive.'

'Well, I'm not going to dismiss it just yet,' I replied. 'But I haven't been able to find anyone with any pressing need to acquire the house. We still have to follow up this lead though. I feel that this could break the case.'

'Maybe you are right. Perhaps we are following it up in the tomorrow.' Basili stood up and looked pointedly at where I was sitting. 'Right now I am most in need of some sleep.'

I stood up, glanced at the door and sat down again.

'Really Mr Harry, I am most very tired. You are going back to your room, yes?'

'Basili, if it's all right with you, I'd prefer to stay here.'

'But why is this, Mr Harry?'

'Your room doesn't have as many spiders as mine. I'd feel much more comfortable sleeping here.'

'But this is a very small bed. There is not enough room for two persons of our size.'

He was right. He'd barely fit in the bed himself. 'I'll just sleep here, in this chair.' I pointed to a very uncomfortable chair in the corner of the room. 'It'll be fine – just try not to fart or snore.'

Basili looked doubtful. 'But Mr Harry, I will be asleep; how will I be controlling myself?'

Now there was a question even I couldn't answer. Briefly I weighed up the alternatives: spiders or flatulent snoring. Yeah, not much in the way of a choice, but in the end staying in Basili's room won – but it was a close contest. Trying to make myself as comfortable as I could in a not-so-comfortable chair, I covered myself with a blanket and settled down (insofar as I could) for a night's sleep.

I don't know how long I'd been sleeping, but it seemed like only minutes before I was awoken by Basili – and not by his snoring. He was shaking me frantically and whispering, 'Wake up Mr Harry. There is being someone outside.'

Blearily, I opened an eye. In the darkness I could make out the ex-genie's huge frame towering over me.

'Wassup? Wha's goin' on?' I mumbled. 'Need sleep.' Before I could turn over, Basili had whipped my blanket away. The sudden draught of cold air over my now-blanketless body brought me to my senses. 'What's going on?' I repeated, wrapping my arms around me in an effort to keep warm.

'Mr Harry, there is much creeping noises outside the room. I am thinking someone is being most careful not to be heard, but my detective senses are picking them up,' Basili announced proudly. 'Are you investigating?'

I noticed the distinct absence of the word 'we' in that last sentence, but chose to ignore it. Shushing Basili, I slid out of the chair, padded to the door and placed my ear against the wood. Basili was right; I could make out the sound of someone shuffling along the landing, doing their best to be undetected. It definitely wasn't the sound that someone having to make an emergency midnight trip to the bathroom would make.

'I'm going to have a look,' I whispered.

'You are being most careful, Mr Harry.' It was probably a warning, but it was also a very accurate statement of my intentions.

I cracked open the door and peered out. The glow of the moon through the web-covered landing window showed a dark shape creeping across the carpet. I couldn't make out who it was, but by their actions, they certainly didn't want to be discovered. Well, it was too late for that. Harry Pigg was on the case and eager to find out who was skulking around Miss Muffet's in the dead of night.

Pushing the door open just enough to let me pass through, I stepped out onto the landing and, tight against the wall, shuffled along after the mysterious stranger. I tried to make out who it might be, but there wasn't enough light. Whoever it was stayed hunched over so it was difficult even to see how tall they were. Then again, I hadn't planned on getting close enough for any kind of physical contest. I just wanted to find out what they were up to (and possibly who they were, as long as I could discover it from a safe distance).

Just as I was contemplating my next move, the shape disappeared from view around a corner where the landing turned to the left, leading to the rest of the guest bedrooms. Maybe we were in for a spot of breaking and entering, though as the stranger was already in the building there wasn't much breaking to be done. Now that I couldn't be seen, I could at least speed up and get to the corner. Tiptoeing along, I'd just come to the turn when an arm reached out, grabbed me around the neck and with a hissed 'Gotcha!' pulled me into the nearest bedroom.

I have a very healthy survival instinct, honed by years of cowardice and reluctance to get involved in any sort of a fight, so when my assailant pushed me to the ground, I rolled away immediately and tried to get to my feet. Before I could do anything I was pushed against a wall, realising at the same time that my reflexes weren't as sharp as I'd hoped – and certainly not as sharp as those of my attacker. Pinned against the unyielding surface, I struggled to break free, but I was held in a grip like a bear-trap.

'All right, let's see who we've got here,' my assailant whispered, reaching for the light switch. At the same time, sensing an opportunity, I pushed as hard as I could and for a second the grip on my throat loosened – but only for a second. Almost immediately I felt a hand grab my hair and heard a grunt of surprise as it came loose in my attacker's grip. Yay for wigs! Anxious to maintain whatever advantage I had, I ducked and threw myself sideways, smacking painfully into a dressing table. Stunned I fell to the ground, unwilling and unable to offer any resistance. I couldn't compete against my attacker and a dressing table. It was two against one, and this one in particular knew when to give up.

I lay on the floor panting and waiting for my attacker (the one that wasn't a dressing table) to finish me off. I was more than a little taken aback when, instead of being either beaten or tied up, the light was switched on and I heard her exclaim, in a very feminine voice, 'Wow, you're one ugly lady.'

Figuring that pointing out I was male might not be the most appropriate response in the circumstances, dressed as I was in ladies' clothes, I heaved myself up into a sitting position and said, 'It's a disguise.'

'And why might someone be staying in this particular guest house disguised as a lady pig?' asked my attacker, who, now that I was getting used to the light, seemed to be a very slim, very attractive and very dangerous-looking woman.

'Maybe for the same reason that another someone is skulking around outside her room, in the dark and trying not to be seen.' Then, in a flash of inspiration, I knew who she was. 'Queenie Harte I presume.'

'Guilty as charged,' she said, raising her hands in admission. 'And you are?'

'Harry Pigg, Private Investigator.'

'Never heard of you.'

'Well, I've never heard of you either. What are you doing here?'

She fumbled in her pocket before producing her ID. 'I'm with the Grimmtown Bureau of Investigation and I'm on a case. What about you?'

'Snap,' I replied. 'But what interest has the GBI in spiders?'

'Spiders? I'm not here because of spiders and the real reason I'm here is none of your business.'

'Well, if you're not telling then I'm not telling either.'

'Okay, be like that. We'll see how secretive you'll be after a night in the cells.'

I was going to point out that it would probably be more comfortable than staying in the B&B, but if I was taken away then there was no chance of cracking the case. 'Your point is well made. Mind if I make myself more comfortable; your floor isn't doing my back any good.'

'Please.' Queenie pointed to another of those uncomfortable armchairs that seemed to be part of every bedroom in the building. Maybe the floor was better after all. I remained there and looked up at Ms Harte. She had obviously gone through her special-agent-doing-undercover-work-at-night checklist: black trainers, black pants and a black top would make her very difficult to see in the dark. She looked like she shopped at SpiesMart.

'Look, I'm here because Miss Muffet asked me to investigate why her premises were being infested with spiders. Initially, I thought someone was trying to put her out of business, but after I discovered who Dad was, I'm fast beginning to think it may be connected to him in some way.' I gave Queenie as sincere a smile as I could. 'Now come on, give me something. I was straight with you. Who knows, I may even be of some help.'

Queenie gave me a disdainful I'm-a-Federal-Agent-how-could-you-possibly-be-of-any-help look, but seemed to relent a little. 'Okay, okay. Here's what I know. Sinbad isn't getting released any time soon. We believe that he hid his fortune somewhere in this house before he was captured and never had a chance to dispose of it properly. He left home when Miss Muffet was very young and hasn't spoken to her since. I think there's bad blood there, so she isn't going to inherit the loot any time soon.

'Now, here's where things get a bit murky. We believe that one or more of the gang members are hoping to double-cross him by trying to find the loot for themselves. With Sinbad locked away, it's an ideal opportunity to make a break for it if they're successful.' Queenie sat on the edge of the bed and sighed. 'As a result, I was sent in to try to integrate myself with the other guests so we could catch the bad guys in the act.' She looked down at me. 'When I heard you following me, I thought I'd got my first break. I knew you weren't for real as soon as I saw you pull up to the front of the house earlier.'

'How?' I asked, my sense of righteous indignation bubbling up.

'Oh, come on, did you really think you could fool anyone with those ridiculous disguises, all that air-kissing and luvvy-this, luvvy-that. There are kids' amateur dramatic groups that are more convincing.'

'Try telling that to the other guests,' I retorted. 'They were falling over themselves to help us finance our latest project. We certainly fooled them.'

'Yes. But, then again, most of the other guests are idiots.'

She had a point.

Something was still nagging at me, though. 'Here's what I don't get. Sinbad has been in prison for the best part of twenty years. So why now? Why wait all this time? It's a bit odd, don't you think?'

'Yeah, we thought that too, until we met George P. Etto.'

'Excuse me? Who's Etto?' I'd never heard of him and wondered how he figured in this.

'Etto was Sinbad's cellmate, in for antiques forgery. He was released about a week ago. Celebrating his new-found freedom he was in the Blarney Tone and, while very drunk, let it slip that Sinbad talked in his sleep. One night Etto had heard him mumble about his fortune, the house and a secret room. 'We believe that somebody, possibly one of Sinbad's gang, heard him, persuaded him, somehow, to be quiet and is now trying to use that information to find the stash.'

I had no illusions about how Etto might have been 'persuaded'. 'And you have no idea which of the guests is the gang member – or if there is more than one?'

Queenie shrugged. 'So far all their stories check out – sort of. The only ones that seem harmless are Mr and Mrs Fussy Eater; all the others are more than a bit dodgy.'

I hadn't had time to really investigate them so now was a good time to get some background information. 'How so?'

'Well, John Nimble is into antiques and is trying to get Miss Muffet to sell her collection of candlesticks, chandeliers and cutlery. We believe he's also a fence and deals with lots of local gangs, helping them to offload stolen goods. So far, though, he seems to be on the level in this particular instance.'

'Okay, that's Nimble. What about Winkie?'

'So far as we're aware, he's just a travelling salesman, but he has a history of breaking and entering. He's gone straight now, or so he says, but that may just be a front.'

'Thomas Piper?'

'Another businessman; buys and sells almost everything. Had a lucrative sideline smuggling animals years ago and did the time.'

'Smuggled animals? So he might be able to lay his hands on a few million spiders?'

'Possibly, but he's been keeping his nose clean these past few years.'

The Curds and Whey Mystery

I made a mental note to check out Piper in more detail. He certainly sounded a likely suspect.

'And then there's Nocchio, self-styled arms dealer.'

I looked up with interest when she said that. 'Arms dealer, now he sounds very shifty.'

Queenie smiled. 'Not really. He also deals in legs, torsos and heads.'

Were we talking about some kind of mass-murderer and, if so, why was he still on the streets? 'Are you serious?' I said.

'Yep, as well as making superb wooden toys and sculptures, he's a supplier of parts to puppeteers and toymakers. He also has quite a reputation for furniture and antiques restoration. Apparently he's quite good. He has a large customer base in Grimmtown. Again, a bit of a shady past. He was involved in that whole Punch and Judy situation. A very messy business. Punch is still doing time.'

So I was no further down the road really. It looked like any of the guests could be responsible for the spiders. I needed some time to think. Reaching for my wig, I stuck it back on my head and ignored Queenie's snigger.

'I'll be heading back to my room now. Goodnight, Ms Harte.'

'Goodnight, Mr Pigg. Or should that be Miss du Crêpe? No doubt I'll see you tomorrow. And if you need some pointers on applying make-up, don't hesitate not to call me.'

I gave her an indignant stare as I marched out the door and back to Basili's bedroom. The look of relief on his face as I closed the door behind me gave me a little reassurance, but I noted that he'd made no effort to follow me and see what had happened.

'Oh, Mr Harriet, I was so worried,' he exclaimed. 'You are being okay, yes?'

I quickly explained what had happened and the newest wrinkle in the case.

'The GBI?' Basili said. 'That is most ominous. Perhaps it would be better if we were leaving things to them.'

'Oh, I don't think so, Basili,' I replied. 'You see, she's not GBI after all.'

'She is not? Now I am being very confused. You have just said that she was.'

'Nope. She said she was, but her ID was as fake as my wig, and I should know, I've used a fair few over the years. I can spot a dodgy ID at fifty paces.'

'But if she is not GBI, then who is this Ms Harte?'

'I don't know yet, but one thing is for sure; she'll need to be watched.'

This case had suddenly become a lot murkier.

10

Breakfast at Matilda's

Next morning, as I sat at the breakfast table, I viewed all the guests in an entirely new light. To be fair, none of them looked remotely suspicious. At a table on their own – which I suspect was deliberate – Licken and Lurkey exchanged bad jokes, practised juggling with their cereal bowls (which meant there was quite a mess around them) and howled hysterically at how funny they were. It was no coincidence that no one else was laughing.

As he placed my fruit bowl in front of me (PAs don't do cereals; calories darling), Jack Horner asked me if there had been any developments. 'Later,' I whispered and he nodded his understanding. Meanwhile, I watched Mr Zingiber as he waited on the other guests. Jack was indeed correct: he was a giant orange cake in the shape of a man, but he didn't seem to let that inhibit him in any way. He served up food and drink with aplomb, but seemed to be especially careful when pouring the guests' tea or coffee. Can't be too careful when you're a gingerbread man I suppose.

This morning I was eating alone, so took the time to go over the events of the day (and night) before. Assuming Queenie Harte was being up front with me, most of the guests had a less than honest reason to be staying in the B&B. Of course, that didn't mean they had motive – it just made them suspicious. If I could connect any of them to the spiders – which seemed to have been fruitful and multiplied overnight, the dining room now looked like it had been caught in a snowstorm – it might just bring me one step closer to cracking the case.

But which one?

I had eliminated Licken and Lurkey as I knew them of old and didn't think they had the sense to pull off a job like this. They might have been rubbish entertainers, but they certainly weren't master criminals. Mr and Mrs Spratt didn't seem like law-breakers either, but I wasn't eliminating them entirely just yet. The rest? Well, take your pick. Any of them could have been the culprit; I just needed to investigate a bit more. Piper was certainly acting strangely. And as for Queenie Harte...

As I sat there staring at the webs on the far wall wafting gently in the breeze, I thought about our encounter the previous night. What brought her here? She certainly wasn't GBI, so who was she – and why was she here? I didn't have any reason to disbelieve what she'd told me about the other guests as she was trying to gain my trust, but anything she said or did from here on would be viewed with suspicion. Of course, this also begged the question: would she be as helpful as she'd promised? I didn't think that, when the chips were down, she was going to be as accommodating as I hoped. Then again, I had no intention of helping her either, so I couldn't really afford to get too precious about it.

Maybe it was time to get to know the guests better. After last night I was at least on second-name terms with most of them, so I figured I had enough to get a chat going. Who knows, maybe they'd let something drop in conversation.

As I speared an apple slice and prepared to eat it, a particularly large spider at the far side of the room caught my eye. He swung from side to side on a tendril of web like an arachnid Tarzan and seemed to be staring at me. If I hadn't known better, I'd have said he was thinking about having me as his next victim – he was certainly scary enough. It was time to nip that in the bud. Grabbing a plum from my bowl, I flung it at the spider. He didn't have time to react before it hit him full on, squashing him against the wooden panel on the wall behind. I smirked as I resumed my breakfast. Pig 1, spider 0.

As I settled back to enjoying my fruit, the spider incident bugged me. I knew I was missing something, but right now, it just wouldn't come. It wouldn't be the first time this had happened, so I figured I'd just let it fester in my head and eventually – usually when I least expected it – it would explode fully formed into my mind, screaming 'look at me, look at me'. Whether it would help me break the case was another thing entirely – it might just as easily turn out to be a recipe for cookies. Well, if it was, Jack would be happy.

'Mind if I join you?' said Willie Winkie, sitting opposite me before I could reply. Pouring himself a coffee, he settled into his chair and looked across the table at me. 'Feeling better?'

For a second I didn't know what he was referring to, until I remembered my little 'episode' from the night before. 'Oh yes, darling, so much better. It's amazing what a good night's sleep can do for one' – as opposed to engaging in a midnight skirmish with a fake GBI agent.

'Good, we were all so worried about you,' Winkie said, without a hint of sincerity.

'Well, I'm fine now and eager to check out this house properly. It has such an ambience don't you think? It's such an ideal location for our movie.'

'Ah, yes, the horror film. What's the plot?'

'Plot?' I was on dangerous ground as I hadn't thought that far ahead. 'Well, um, some kids – we have some of the finest child actors lined up already – creep into a haunted house in the middle of the night and scary things start happening to them.'

'Like what?'

'Ghosts, things that go bump in the night, that sort of thing.'

'You know, it's funny you should mention bumps in the night. I could have sworn I heard noises outside my room after I went to bed. I think that's what woke me up.'

'And did you find out what was making them?' I asked, trying not to look as guilty as I felt.

'Nah, I just put it down to the age of the house. In a place like this you must expect lots of funny noises.'

'And speaking of the house, if you don't mind my asking, what convinced you to stay here?' I waved my trotters at the cobwebs. 'It's hardly the most comfortable.'

'It's a bit unorthodox, I'll grant you,' he replied. 'But it's cheap and, more importantly, it's very close to the Rag District.'

'Excuse me? Rag District?'

'Yes, where all the clothes shops are. That's my business you see, I sell clothing; in particular, I deal in nightwear: dressing gowns, pyjamas, nightgowns, that sort of thing. In fact, if you're looking for costumes for your film, I might just be able to sort you out with a good deal.'

'Ah, that won't be necessary, our Costume Department look after that kind of thing. Anyway, I don't think there'll be much need for nightwear in this movie.'

'But you've said it takes place at night, so you never know,' Winkie replied. He was certainly persistent.

'Tell you what, I'll take it up with the producers; see what they say.'

'I'd be grateful.'

'So,' I said, putting my metaphorical detective's hat back on. 'Have you been in the clothes business for long?'

'Yep, I'm an old hand at it now. I started off with a small stall in Grimmtown Market and built it up from there.'

'I imagine in the sales game you must meet all kinds of interesting people.'

'Over the years I've met all sorts. Maybe if we get an opportunity later, I could tell you a few stories.'

Oh, yes, now that would be fun: listening to a travelling salesman bore me to tears with his tales of tailors and seamstresses. 'Well, Mr Schmidt-Heye is toying with making another documentary after he finishes his horror movie. He's looking at Grimmtown's criminal underworld and its characters. You must have come across a few in your time.'

Was it my imagination or did a shifty expression cross Winkie's face?

'To tell the truth,' he stammered, 'I've been very lucky. I've never bumped into anyone shady in my years selling clothes.'

'Oh, I do find that hard to believe, darling. Surely you're being far too modest. A man of your wide-ranging experience must have encountered a shady character or two.'

'No, not really. As I said, I've been lucky.' He stood up from the table. 'Now if you'll excuse me, I really must be going.'

'But you haven't finished your coffee,' I pointed out.

'I'll take it with me,' he said, grabbing the mug in both hands and almost dropping it again it was so hot. 'The caffeine helps me focus.'

Not to mention your burnt hands, I thought. 'Have a good day.'

Well, he had started acting very strangely once the conversation veered into the criminal. Then again, that didn't necessarily make him guilty. He would need further investigation though. Spotting Jack serving at another table, I waved him over and pointed at Winkie as he disappeared out the door.

'See that guy?' I asked.

Jack nodded. 'Yes, that's Mr Winkie.'

'I want you to follow him and see where he goes. Be careful and make sure he doesn't see you.'

'I'll be the invisible man,' Jack replied, proud to have been given a real mission.

'I don't doubt it,' I said.

As Jack scurried off after his target I watched the other guests. Mr and Mrs Spratt were dividing up their bacon, Thomas Piper was pretending to read the paper, but I could see his head move back and forth as he followed Miss Muffet's movements in and out of the room as she served breakfast. At a separate table, Nocchio and Nimble were deep in conversation. In fact, from where I sat it looked like they were having an argument. Detecting antennae went on full alert as I stood up and edged towards them, in the guise of getting a newspaper from the rack on the wall beside them. As casually as I could, I stood within hearing distance and pretended to scan the front page.

'No, ees madness,' Nocchio whispered, staring at Nimble.

'What choice do we have?' Nimble replied. 'It has to be done now.'

'But 'ow? We don't know where eet is.'

Now that could quite easily be a conversation about Sinbad's fortune. Had I finally got a break in the case?

'But we'll find it soon, I know it.' Nimble spotted me hovering and waved at Nocchio to be quiet.

'Morning daaaarlings,' I bluffed. 'And how are we all this glorious morning?'

'Fine, fine,' Nimble blustered and Nocchio nodded agreement.

'Great. Well I have a location to examine, so I'll see you darling gentlemen later. Time is money you know.' I made my way back to my table and finished my breakfast, mulling over what I'd just heard. Winkie might have been shifty, but the conversation I'd just eavesdropped upon was downright dodgy. Those two gentlemen would warrant further observation – but they were now looking suspiciously across the room at me, so I figured they'd be very careful around me. I needed someone else to do the listening.

Just as I was mulling over my dilemma, Queenie Harte strode into the room and made for a table in the corner. The best way to keep an eye on her would be to invite her to share my table. As she was oblivious to the fact that her cover had been blown, I might even be able to get more information out of her. It meant sharing what I'd seen this morning, but I figured it was worth the trade-off.

'Ms Harte. Oh, Ms Harte, would you care to join me, darling? We haven't had a chance to talk yet.'

Queenie glanced over her shoulder at me and would probably have ignored my request had I not made it out loud. Unwilling to be seen to be anti-social in front of all the other guests, she sat down in the seat recently vacated by Willie Winkie. 'It's Ms du Crêpe isn't it? We haven't been formally introduced, but I'm aware of your charge's reputation. It's a pleasure to meet you.' The expression on her face suggested otherwise, but I didn't care.

'Ms Harte, the feeling's mutual. Please, have some breakfast.' I waved Mr Zingiber over and he carefully filled Queenie's cup with hot coffee. As she sipped, I updated her on the morning's events. To my surprise, she didn't seem too interested in what I'd overheard.

'Come on,' she said. 'They could have been talking about anything.'

'Maybe. But considering our current situation, don't you think it might have some bearing on the case?'

'It's possible, I suppose.' She mulled it over as she drank. 'But I'm not going to waste time on something that might just turn out to be a red herring.'

She seemed very casual about it. I wondered if she had something more important to do – something that she was keeping from me despite our conversation of the night before. Yes, I know, I'd have done the same, but that didn't make it any easier to stomach.

'You know something, don't you?' I jabbed a trotter at her. 'Something you're not telling me.'

'Of course I don't. Don't be ridiculous. I told you last night that I'd pass on any information, didn't I?'

'You did, but I'm starting to think you might have been leading me on.' I stood up from the table. 'Anyway, I've more important things to be doing.' In the interests of keeping up appearances, I walked around and air-kissed her (I was getting quite good at it by now), whispering at the same time, 'If I find you've kept something from me, I'll —'

'You'll what?' she snapped. 'Remember who you're talking to. If I want I can have you detained for obstruction of justice. You wouldn't do too much investigating then, would you?'

I stepped back, pretending to be suitably chastened. 'You're right, of course.' I bowed my head in mock-humility. 'Carry on with whatever you're doing. I'll just scoot off and scout locations for the day, shall I?'

'Yes, you carry on with your PA work. I'm sure you're very good at it.' Queenie's voice dripped sarcasm, but I ignored it. Better people than her have been sarcastic towards me, so she'd have to be really good to get any kind of response. I left the table and went upstairs to Basili's room. I'd instructed him to order room service and wait until I got back – it was a form of damage limitation. By now I was beginning to think that our cover story wasn't quite as well thought out as we had originally planned. Maybe next time we'd just go in as ordinary guests (in disguise, of course). Well, they do say hindsight is 20-20 vision and, based on our current success rate, we must have been very short-sighted.

I was just about to knock on the door when I spotted something on the floor. It was lying where the carpet met the wall and must have been missed by the cleaning staff – although if the cleaning staff amounted to one gingerbread man then it would be easy to see why. Curious, I bent down and picked it up. It looked like a raisin but had a rubbery texture. I was still examining it when I entered the room.

Basili was still there, stretched out on the bed.

'Have you any plans to get up today?' I asked, rolling the strange object around in my trotter.

'But of course, Mr Harry. I am waiting for you to be returning so we can discuss our strategy.' Basili got off the bed and began dressing in character once more.

'Ah, strategy. Here's where we are: Jack is following Willie Winkie to see if he's on the level. Nocchio and Nimble looked to be having a row at the breakfast table, Thomas Piper is watching everything Miss Muffet does and Queenie Harte is threatening to put me in jail. There, have I covered everything?' I had briefed Basili about my encounter with Queenie the night before, after I arrived back at the bedroom bruised, tired and with my wig askew. The ex-genie contemplated what I'd said, nodded sagely and said...well...nothing.

'That's it, that's all you have to offer: a nod?' I screeched.

Basili had the decency to blush. 'I am most sorry, Mr Harry. There is nothing that I am offering at this moment. I am sure that I am being most disappointing to you, particularly when our small friend, young Jack, is being a most practical detective.' He looked curiously at what I had in my hand. 'And what is that you are playing with?'

I looked at the object again just as Basili sat at the dressing table and began to dab some make-up on his face. As he did so, my brain finally decided to wake up properly and start making connections.

Make-up; rubbery raisin-like object.

'It's a wart, Basili,' I said.

'That is very disgusting. Why are you playing with such a thing?'

Oh, it's not a real wart. It's fake. Someone else in this house has been disguising themselves. And what kind of person might have a wart?'

'Ah.' The ex-genie's face lit up. 'An orcy person. You are thinking that perhaps someone is making the disguise and visiting the froggy man to buy his spiders?'

'That's exactly what I'm thinking.' And I was thinking very hard indeed. Things were starting to come together at last. Basili's comment about Jack, the fake wart, the guests and Frogg Prince's statement all began to link together in my head. There might be more of the guests involved in the crime, but I was starting to narrow down my list of definite suspects. At last I had something to go on.

11

A Secret Revealed

Leaning forward, I kissed Basili on the forehead. 'You're a genius,' I said to the puzzled ex-genie. 'I think we may finally have a breakthrough.'

'I am? We do?' Basili didn't know whether to preen or be confused. 'Perhaps you are explaining it to me.'

'Well, remember Frogg Prince's description of the orc that came into the store?'

Basili's face was a study in concentration. 'He was saying that it was a most unpleasant creature: very smelly, very green and with a wart.'

'Yes, but he also described him as being small, remember? And how many small guests are staying here at the moment?'

I could see Basili counting them out one by one. 'Two?' he ventured.

'Exactly. Jack Spratt and Willie Winkie. Everyone else is just too tall.'

'But Mr Spratt is being such a jolly person.'

'Indeed, but that's why you should never let emotion get in the way of good detecting. Everyone is a suspect until proven otherwise.' I was still finding it hard to believe Jack Spratt could be involved in this. Basili was right in that respect: he just didn't seem the type. But now that he was a likely suspect I'd have to pay more attention to him – and possibly even his wife. The 'perfect 10' would now be under my unwavering gaze from here on in as well. So many suspects, so few eyes. It was very possible that I'd have to enlist Basili in taking a more active role in the day-to-day operations of the Agency, though I shuddered to think of him trying to shadow a suspect. It wouldn't be shadowing so much as a total eclipse. The only way he'd manage to stay unseen would be if someone managed to cast an invisibility spell on him – and even then he'd probably end up barging people out of the way like a mini-hurricane as he followed his target down the street. He certainly wouldn't be unobtrusive.

'You know, it's a bit stuffy in here.' I headed towards the window and pushed it open. Considering two of us had slept in the room (or tried to sleep, in my case), one of whom suffered from flatulence, fresh air was very much the order of the morning. A cool breeze wafted through the window, blowing the cobwebs that were evidence of the spiders' attempt to reconquer the room. Some of the strands floated across the room and settled against the wall on the far side.

As they drifted to the floor, my brain, already fully charged having sorted out the disguised orc issue, decided to go for broke and head for a touchdown. Why did the webs moving suggest something to me?

Wafting webs.

Webs in a draught.

Just like those I'd seen in the dining room at breakfast – which were nowhere near any draught from the door. Something else had made them move. Maybe air escaping from something like a hidden door or secret passage.

My brain hit the end-zone and the crowd went crazy. 'Basili.' I grabbed the ex-genie and hauled him to his feet. 'Get ready to act like you've never acted before. I think I know where Sinbad's fortune is hidden, but I need you to get everyone out of the dining room.'

To his credit, Basili didn't ask any stupid questions – for a change. He finished dressing in his Acme Director's Outfit™, flicked some imaginary dust off his shoulders, straightened his back and got back in character.

'Mr Schmidt-Heye will be looking most very hard for some actors for his most magnificent movie. Perhaps I am holding auditions in the lounge.'

And by extension, no one would be in the dining room while I investigated the wafting webs.

'Basili, you're excelling yourself today – and it's still only morning,' I said, thumping him on the back. 'We might make a detective of you yet.'

'I am learning much from such an excellent tutor as yourself,' he said proudly. I didn't doubt it; with someone like me to learn from, even Basili could pick up a tip or two.

Now it was time to see if all his learning could be put to some practical field use – and, more importantly, would he be able to carry it off on his own. I needed him to keep the guests distracted while he remained in character. It was a big ask and, to tell the truth, I was more than a bit apprehensive. He wouldn't have me to interfere for him, or be there to prompt him if he ran into difficulty. He needed to be Alain Schmidt-Heye and to do so he'd have to ignore all my advice of the previous day; he'd be talking for an extended period of time and I suspected there would be a certain amount of physical contact. Well, it couldn't be helped; he was on his own and there was nothing I could do about it.

After passing on a few last minute tips I headed downstairs into the dining room, took up what I hoped was a casual pose at the mantelpiece and waited, casually ignoring everybody and trying to look superior. Fortunately, Basili swung into action immediately, so no sooner had I adopted Superior Look No. 7 – I'm in the Movie Industry and You're Not, Insignificant Worm – than there was a loud thumping as he tested the stairs' tolerance limits with his feet as he descended and headed into the lounge.

'Can I have everyone's attention please,' I ordered – as opposed to asking (PAs don't ask). 'Mr Schmidt-Heye is not only extremely excited about the ambience of these premises, but he also feels that, as sometime residents, having you in the movie might add to the overall sense of realism that he is striving for. Accordingly, he will be holding auditions for the role of guests, starting,' I glanced at my watch, 'well, now actually.'

There was a stunned silence followed almost immediately by a mass exodus. Ah, the lure of the movies, I thought. It gets 'em every time. Even Mr and Mrs Spratt had gone out for a look.

I scanned the room once more, just to be sure it was empty, and turned to where I'd seen the webs move. As I studied them, they once more fluttered gently in a breeze of some description. My initial hunch was correct: it wasn't a draught from the door. Something else was definitely blowing the webs. I ran my trotters along the wooden panels beside the fireplace. At first I thought I'd been mistaken, but I felt it on my second pass: a gentle gust emanating from what seemed to be a slender vertical crack in one of the panels. It didn't look like natural wear and tear, which suggested only one thing to my rapier-like mind: a secret passage of some description. All I had to do now was figure out the mechanism to open it.

Of course, I'd come across secret doors, passages and tunnels before and had built up quite an expertise in figuring out how to open them – which was just as well as Basic Techniques 1–3 (pushing, pressing and pulling) failed miserably. Conscious that someone was eventually going to come back into the room, I moved onto Techniques 4–7 (finding a trigger, cracking a combination, solving a mysterious message and my own addition to the pantheon: hitting everything and hoping for the best). To my surprise (and the bruising of my ego) none of the classic steps worked. I was figuring that maybe there wasn't a secret passage there at all when, as I stepped back for a better look, I stumbled over the fire irons. Grabbing at anything that might keep me upright, my trotters gripped onto a circular carving cut into the stonework of the fireplace itself. Instead of offering support, it twisted under the pressure and, as I hit the ground, I was rewarded with the sound of wood scraping on wood as the panel slid aside to reveal a dark space behind. Forgetting about my injured dignity, I stood up and peered cautiously into the opening. It did occur to me as I did so that Sinbad's fortune, if that was indeed what was hidden behind the panel, wasn't going to amount to much as the secret passage was barely bigger than a cereal carton and not really large enough to store more than a gold bar or two.

In fact, now that I could see into it, there wasn't any gold inside either. A small wooden box nestled snugly in the hole. It didn't look like much; no runes, mysterious carvings or strange inscriptions. By the same token, it didn't look booby-trapped either.

It wouldn't be long before I wouldn't be on my own any more. Throwing any hint of caution aside, I grabbed the box and pulled it out waiting for the explosion, release of gas, or some strategically placed spring-loaded metal spike to assail me. When none of the above occurred, I cracked the lid on the box and pushed it ever-so-carefully open. Inside there wasn't a treasure map, nor a letter from Sinbad, and there certainly wasn't any treasure. Nestling snugly on a velvet cushion was a small blue bean. More importantly, it wasn't a runner bean, green bean, baked bean or kidney bean. I recognised the sparkly aura that surrounded it; it was the type of aura that screamed 'I'm a magic bean. Look at me and observe my magnificence and my suggestion of things occult.' Any time I came across any kind of magic object, I much preferred to observe its suggestion of things occult from a safe distance – preferably another continent – and this particular magic artifact was no exception. I've made no secret in the past of my hatred of all things magic as, when they got involved in my cases, things generally didn't turn out well. Looking at the particular magic bean posing proudly in its case, I figured this would be no exception.

I'd like to say that I wasn't surprised then, when I heard a voice behind me whisper, 'Thank you so very much, kind lady. I knew there was more to you than met the eye.' Before I could react, there was a sharp smack to the back of my head and I stumbled forward, striking the front of it against the mantelpiece. Faced with a double-whammy of head trauma, my system decided enough was enough and slowly began to shut itself down as I slid to the floor. The last thing

I saw before I blacked out completely was a gloved hand taking the box from my trotter.

12

Bean There, Done That

B asili was bending over me, shaking me (a bit too violently for trying to wake up someone who'd just been mugged, I thought).

'Mr Harry...I mean Miss du Crêpe, are you okay?' Now he was trying to drag me to my feet. Did he know nothing about the basics of first aid?

I waved him away. 'I'm fine,' I mumbled. 'Just give me some space.' My head ached all over courtesy of the symmetrical strikes it had received, my vision was blurred and I think my skirt had ridden up over my thighs. I quickly tugged it back down to a more acceptable level before worrying about my physical well-being. A girl's got priorities after all. 'Who else is here?'

'Oh, no one. I have given them all a scene to prepare. They are being most busy with the rehearsals, so I am taking a five before I am having to return. I was being most concerned when I saw you on the floor.'

The mugging was coming into clearer focus now. 'Basili, when you were talking to the guests, were they all there, or did anyone leave during your act?'

The ex-genie mulled it over for a second before giving me a rueful stare. 'I am sorry, I am not really noticing.' As he spoke he seemed to observe something. Raising his head he sniffed the air carefully.

'What is it, Basili? What can you smell?'

'There has been some apparatus of magic in this vicinity very most recently,' he said. 'I can sense it.'

Of course, being an ex-genie he could probably detect the lingering aura of the magic bean. Quickly I explained about what I'd found and he nodded his head. 'Yes, that is it. Definitely pulse magic. Very powerful.'

I reached into my handbag, grabbed my phone and punched in a number.

'Good morning, Directory Enquiries, how may I be of assistance?'

'I need you to put me through to Beanstalk Control right away,' I demanded.

'Of course, sir, please hold the line.' There was a brief pause followed by the number being connected.

'This is Beanstalk Control. For details of licensed beanstalks in your area, please press 1 now. For details on how to register your beanstalk, please press 2 now. For help with beanstalk removal, please press 3 now. For information on unregulated beanstalks in your area, please press 4 now.'

I punched 4 on my keypad and waited.

'Your call is important to us. Please hold and a Beanstalk Engineer will take your call as soon as one becomes available.' Seconds later a sanitised version of one of Hubbard's Cubbard's very early hits, sounding like it was being played by a hippo on a toy keyboard, came down the line – presumably to help me relax while I waited for the next available Beanstalk Engineer. I ground my teeth in frustration while listening to how important to Beanstalk Control my call was; all the while wondering was it actually possible that so many people with unlicensed beanstalk issues had called at exactly the same time, thus putting everyone else on hold.

'Come on, come on,' I muttered. 'I don't have time for this.' Then I noticed something: was it as a result of my injuries or did the dining room seem darker? Before I could consider it further, Beanstalk Control finally decided that I was, in fact, actually important to them after all and assigned an operative to my call.

'Hi, this is Fred in Unlicensed Beanstalks. Thank you for your patience and understanding. How can I help you today?'

'Well, Fred, I was wondering if there have been any reports of unlicensed beanstalks in the Grimmtown area this morning?' I asked.

'Just a moment, sir, and I'll check,' Fred put me on hold once more while he went off to investigate. This time, however, I wasn't waiting long. 'Yes, sir, in fact we have reports of one such plant this morning and – whoa, it's a biggie. I don't think I've seen one that big since—'

As he spoke I suddenly understood why exactly the room had become darker. A large shape outside the window was blocking most of the light. 'Thanks, Fred, you've been a great help,' I said.

'But don't you want to know where it is?' Fred was being a true professional right to the end.

'It's okay, Fred, I think I have a fair idea.' Outside the dining room window, I could make out a giant leaf and part of what I now knew to be a beanstalk trunk. This particular plant was in Miss Muffet's backyard. Whoever had taken the bean from me had acted fast.

I was just on the point of hanging up when I thought of another – and very vital – question. 'Where's this particular plant going to?'

'Ah, now there's an interesting thing: it's going all the way to Neringus's Castle.'

Now at this point I need to present a little Beanstalk 101. Most of you probably already know that they grow from magic beans, extend quite a bit into the sky and are tricky to both climb up and chop down. What you probably don't realise is that these beanstalks connect to a number of cloud kingdoms, mostly small ones, that hover in the skies over

Grimmtown. As a result, all beanstalks are both registered and licensed with the good folk of Beanstalk Control to ensure both the safety of air-traffic above the city and to control access to these cloud kingdoms. The people in these aerial fiefdoms – usually giants – have an arrangement with Grimmtown Corporation: in return for prompt payment of taxes they are assured of privacy and managed access via registered beanstalks. As you can imagine, they aren't overly keen on tourists and prefer that most other people – especially brave young adventurers – just stay away. In fact, if one was to hide a large treasure trove, a kingdom in the clouds would be the perfect place – assuming one of their rulers let you enter in the first place. Then again, if treasure was involved, chances were a small bribe might help those selfsame rulers get over any rampant xenophobia they might have and allow it to be stashed somewhere safe.

Bearing that in mind, if Sinbad's fortune was in Neringus's Castle, he couldn't have picked a safer place to stash it. That particular edifice hovered in the highest section of clouds above Grimmtown. This made it difficult to get to in normal circumstances. On top of that, it was ruled by a particularly unpleasant member of the giant community named Neringus. Usual advice, where he was concerned, was to stay well away. Stories abounded – some probably true – of those above-mentioned brave young adventurers who fancied their chances against him only to find that legends didn't always tell the whole truth and favour the small guy. Apparently, back in the old days it was a common occurrence to find bits of the more unsuccessful adventurers raining from the sky after the latest failed quest – so much so that Grimmtown Police Department placed a blanket ban on any further expeditions to the clouds, after a particularly unpleasant experience when the mayor of Grimmtown was hit on the head by a falling leg while giving an outdoor speech on pollution and the importance of clean air.

If deciding what to do once you got to a cloud kingdom – apart from actually staying alive – was a problem, getting there was fraught with even more difficulty. The only approved access was beanstalks, which was all very well if you were young, fit and able to climb for extended periods of time. All aerial transport in and around them was banned and the ban was strictly enforced: on the ground by Beanstalk Control, through legislation, and in the air by the giants – usually through shooting down any aircraft that wandered too close. The giants' method was generally considered to be the more effective of the two, and that was causing me no end of concern as I left the B&B to take a look at the beanstalk.

As beanstalks went it was a particularly fine example of the species. Shooting out of the ground where the magic bean had been planted, it towered above us, twisting its way into the sky to disappear from view among the clouds. Giant leaves the size of cars shaded us from the sun and the plant's trunk was as wide as the house beside it. I took one look at its size and knew there was no way I was climbing it. For one thing, climbing is murder when you have trotters and, more importantly, I wasn't was as young as I used to be; even if I managed to get a foothold I'd probably only make a few feet before giving up in pain and exhaustion, with very sore legs.

Beside me Basili looked apprehensively at the towering green structure. 'We will not be climbing that, Mr Harry?' His gaze stretched up further. 'Will we?'

'I don't think so, Basili, but, as always, I have a plan.' I pulled out my phone and made a quick call. 'Ali, it's me, Harry. I need another favour and this time I promise it'll be the last one.'

'If you say so, Harry,' came the weary voice from the other end. 'What is it this time?'

'I need to borrow another of your carpets; one of the long-range ones that can travel at altitude.'

'And where would this particular magic carpet be travelling to?'

'Well, we have a new beanstalk in town and I need to get to the top.'

Ali Baba laughed. 'No chance, Harry. None of my carpets – in fact no magic carpet – is capable of travelling at that altitude. They're just not designed for it. And even if they were, there's no way I'd lend you one. It wouldn't last five minutes once it got up there. Those giants aren't too friendly, you know.'

'You think? Okay, thanks anyway, Ali.' I turned to Basili. 'Well, scratch that plan. We won't be travelling by magic carpet this time.'

'So, how will we be getting there?' asked the perplexed ex-genie.

'That, my good friend, is an excellent question and one to which I still haven't figured out an answer,' I replied, looking once more at the intimidating mass of greenery that stretched into the sky above.

'Well, I am most confident that you will, very, very soon,' Basili said, and he placed a comforting arm around my shoulders.

I was encouraged by my partner's confidence in me, but I still had no idea how to get to the top of the beanstalk. Any aircraft we might use would probably be blown out of the sky before we got near it.

Then other, more important short-term thoughts struck me. Who had planted the magic bean? And, having planted it, had they climbed up to the clouds above? Well, there was an easy way to find out.

'Basili, stay here and get into character again. I need to get everyone out here to see who's not around any more.'

'But of course, Mr Harry,' Basili replied. 'I will be ready.'

I rushed back into the house and shouted, 'Mr Schmidt-Heye has been most impressed with your performances. We've set up an outdoor set for some more testing, so if you could all step outside into the garden that would be lovely.'

The Curds and Whey Mystery

There was a flurry of bodies as the guests decamped *en masse* outdoors. 'Anyone left inside?' I screamed. 'Anyone else want to do a screen test.'

'There's no one left here,' said an unfamiliar voice behind me. I spun around to face Zingiber, the gingerbread manservant. 'They're all outside now. All that's left here are the staff.' Turning his back on me, he skulked back towards the kitchen.

'Charming,' I muttered, as I made my way back outside once more.

In the garden, the guests were swarming around, gazing up at the beanstalk and chattering excitedly. 'Gosh,' said John Nimble. 'That's a most elaborate set; how did you set it up so quickly?' He slapped the nearest leaf. 'Wow, it feels so lifelike.'

'That's set designers for you,' I said. 'They work fast and try to make it as real as possible.' I looked around the garden, checking off the guests as I went along. I'd just seen Nimble and had checked Queenie Harte off my list on the basis of the previous night's activities. Thomas Piper was talking to Pietro Nocchio and Miss Muffet, and Mr and Mrs Spratt were examining the beanstalk with interest. Maybe they were figuring out how best to eat it. That only left Willie Winkie, who was being tailed by Jack Horner and wasn't even in the building when I'd been attacked.

Now I was confused. I'd eliminated all the guests and there was still no sign of who had stolen the magic bean.

Or had I?

As I stood there something fluttered down from the beanstalk and came to a halt at my feet. I looked down at a large white chicken feather and realised that I'd badly miscalculated. I'd never even considered Licken and Lurkey as possible culprits because I figured they weren't bright enough and I'd known them for years. I'd been misled. Now that fowl duo were climbing the beanstalk, trying to get to the top and lay their hands on Sinbad's treasure.

There had to be some way of getting there before them; there just had to be. Maybe someone could cast a magic spell and teleport me there. Basili quickly poured water on that particular scheme. 'All cloud kingdoms have a magic-damping field around them to prevent the very thing that you are being suggesting, Mr Harry. There is, of course, much magic once you arrive, but alas it cannot be used to get there.'

Well, scratch that as a plan. Unless I came up with something quickly, Licken and Lurkey would get away, but what could I do? Just as despair began to creep over me a thought struck me: 'maybe the (fake) GBI could be of assistance.'

Queenie Harte had slid up beside me.

'What can the GBI do to get to the top of the beanstalk? Do you have super-fast climbers or something?'

'I'm afraid not,' Queenie replied. 'We'd need to go through channels, just like everyone else.'

The Curds and Whey Mystery

Then an offer of help came from a most surprising source.

'I think I might be of some assistance,' smiled Miss Muffet. 'Just wait here, I'll be right back.'

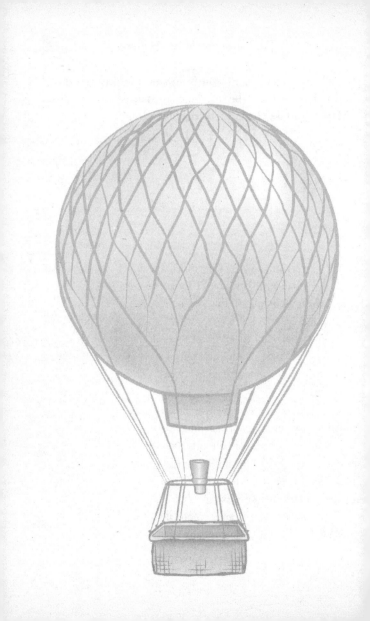

13
Lots of Hot Air

'**A**re you crazy?' I said to Miss Muffet. 'This has no chance of working.' I looked disbelievingly at the hot-air balloon that was being prepped for take-off as I spoke.

'Oh, yes it will,' Miss Muffet replied. 'My father used to use them when he needed to approach the cloud kingdoms under the radar, so to speak.'

I remembered the picture of Sinbad in the hot-air balloon that had adorned the stairway wall. 'But how?' I asked. 'Any unauthorised aircraft approaching them is destroyed.'

'That's the beauty of balloons,' Miss Muffet said. 'Firstly, they're quiet. Secondly, if they ascend close to the beanstalk they don't usually get detected. The beanstalk's own mass helps to mask their approach.'

'Usually,' I interrupted. 'You said "don't usually get detected". What does that mean exactly?'

'Well, it doesn't always work,' Miss Muffet replied with a rueful expression. 'Sometimes the balloons get caught in the branches; other times they stray too far from the beanstalk's cover and get detected; but I'm an excellent pilot, I don't think that will happen to us.'

I know I sounded like I was just repeating everything she said, but everything she said was setting off alarm bells inside my head. 'And what exactly do you mean by "get detected"?'

'If we're not on any approved flight list then they'll probably just shoot us down,' she replied. 'But that's unlikely to happen.'

'"Unlikely to happen"?' Yes, I was doing it again. 'Unlikely how?'

'Look, I know what I'm doing. They won't know we're there. Trust me.'

I wished I shared her confidence. The last thing I needed was an angry giant gunning (possibly quite literally) for me while I floated around in a very big, very obvious and very defenceless target.

'And there's no other way,' I asked, resigned to the inevitable answer.

Miss Muffet shook her head. 'Not if you want to get there now. If we have to go through official channels and get approved flight plans, visas and travel permits we'll be tied up in paperwork for days. By then the culprits will have gone to ground and we'll never find that treasure.' She turned and looked at the balloon. The red globe was filling with hot air and struggled against the guy ropes that were securing it to the ground. 'Oh, look, it's nearly inflated. Time to get on board.'

'You're absolutely sure about this?' I asked as I nervously approached the basket that would be keeping us safe for the duration of the trip – a very delicate and fragile-looking basket, I have to add.

'Absolutely; we'll be as safe as an...um...ah...very safe thing,' Miss Muffet said as she clambered up the rope ladder that dangled from the basket's edge. Her reply did nothing to reassure me.

'Are you getting in, or what?' she shouted from above.

'Just a moment,' I said. 'I need to do something first.' I rushed back into the B&B, up to my room and grabbed my case. Seconds later I was out of my costume and back in my detective's clothes. Well, my cover had been blown anyway; I might as well get comfortable. Glad to be wearing civvies once more, I ran back to the balloon where an agitated Miss Muffet was waiting impatiently.

'Hurry up, we haven't got all day.'

I gritted my teeth, muttered, 'Here goes nothing,' and ascended the rope ladder, only managing to get tied up in it twice before dropping into the basket.

Inside it was a lot roomier than it looked from the ground. Clearly Sinbad hadn't skimped on his comforts when in the field (or over it in this case). A carpeted floor was covered with cushions and seatbelts hung loosely from the walls. A small control desk allowed someone to pilot the craft and the burner that heated the air, keeping the balloon airborne, spurted flame over my head.

'It's certainly a bit more snug than a magic carpet,' I said as I sat down and strapped myself in.

'Nothing but the best for my father,' said Miss Muffet.

As I made myself comfortable, I became aware of raised voices from outside the balloon.

'No,' said one. 'You can't go; it's too dangerous.'

'Oh, yes I can,' replied Jack Horner. 'Harry needs me. I'm the one who keeps him out of trouble.'

'And I am being flying too,' said an indignant Basili from outside, also getting in on the act. 'Please be standing aside.'

Although I couldn't see what was going on, I didn't imagine anyone was going to stand in Basili's way. No one's life would be worth that. Minutes later, after much huffing and puffing, he fell into the basket, followed almost immediately by a very happy Jack Horner.

'Well, the gang's all here,' he said excitedly as he looked around.

'Indeed we are,' I said. 'It's good to see you again. How did you get on following Willie Winkie?'

Jack's face dropped. 'It was really boring. He just wandered around clothes shops talking to people and shaking their hands. Next time give me something more interesting to do.'

'I'll see what I can find.' I rubbed his head affectionately. 'At least your work may have helped eliminate him from our enquiries.'

Jack's face lit up. 'It did? Wow.'

I shifted around on my cushion and asked Miss Muffet when we'd be airborne.

'Any second now,' she said.

There was more commotion from outside the basket.

'Let me through,' roared a man's voice. 'I need to be on that balloon.'

I looked over the side and saw Thomas Piper furiously pushing people out of his way as he raced towards the ladder.

'I'd suggest we leave now,' I said. 'I don't know what his problem is, but I'd prefer that he not come with us.'

'Right you are,' said Miss Muffet, and she released the moorings. There was a lurch and the balloon began to ascend. With a roar of frustration, Piper leaped up to grab onto the ladder and missed it by inches. He waved his fist angrily at me as the balloon gathered speed. I refrained from waving back – or making any other gestures either.

'Why is the Piper gentleman so eager to ascend with us?' Basili asked. 'Does he like balloons?'

'I have no idea,' I said. 'But based on his behaviour since we arrived in the B&B, I don't want him here with us.'

Jack stood up to look over the edge of the basket. 'Look at Miss Muffet's. From up here it looks tiny.'

I wasn't too concerned with events on the ground; I was far more worried about the giant green plant that seemed to be far too near us. Miss Muffet was taking the 'flying close to the beanstalk' tactic as literally as she could. If I stretched out my hand I'd be able to grab a leaf.

'This isn't too bad,' she said, spotting my concern. 'There are no dangerous air currents and we're ascending nicely. We should be at the top before too much longer.'

'And what then?' I asked. 'A balloon will hardly be inconspicuous poking above the clouds.'

'Ah, but it won't be going above the clouds.' Miss Muffet made some adjustments to the balloon's ascent. 'Once we reach the top, we'll moor ourselves to the beanstalk just below cloud level and finish the journey on foot. There will probably be an immigration post that we'll have to avoid; other than that I don't envisage any problems.'

No, apart from hiding a large hot-air balloon, navigating a beanstalk thousands of feet above the ground and avoiding immigration security on a cloud. No problem at all.

I was enjoying the quiet and resisting all temptation to check out the scenery below and above when, as is usual with these things, events began to take a turn for the worse.

'Uh – oh,' announced Jack. 'That doesn't look too good.'

'What? What doesn't?' I scrambled to my feet and looked in the direction Jack was pointing. Heading towards the balloon at great speed and with deadly intent was a flock of birds with what looked to be very sharp beaks.

'Well, they're not coming to escort us,' said Miss Muffet. She caught me by the arm and pulled me over to the controls. 'Here, you pilot.'

'M-m-me? I don't know how to drive a balloon.' I looked blankly at the small control panel.

'There's nothing to it, just keep an eye on those dials and if we start to veer off course or to descend, just fire off the burner there.'

'What will you be doing during all this?'

'Attending to our visitors,' Miss Muffet replied, grimly, as she opened a long wicker box at the side of the control panel and took out a very mean-looking crossbow. 'Unfortunately, I don't have too many bolts so I hope there aren't too many birds out there.'

She took up position beside Jack, loaded a bolt and took aim. I wasn't able to watch – not because I was frightened, although I was – but because I needed to keep the balloon steady. I used Jack's shouting as an indication of how successful Miss Muffet's aim was.

'Got him, good shot.' Well, that was positive. One down already.

'Oooh, unlucky, you just missed him.' Not so good. 'But not that time.' She was obviously a good shot.

'Quick, now they're flying around to the other side.' The balloon lurched as the other three rushed around to that side of the basket.

'Oh, another good shot, Miss Muffet. You're great at this.' Frankly, I was hoping she was. All it would take was one sharp-beaked bird to evade the crossbow bolts and we would be in big trouble.

Seconds later we were in big trouble.

'Shoot! shoot!' shouted Jack.

'Dammit,' grunted Miss Muffet, which I took to mean she'd missed.

'Oh dear,' said Basili, and this was followed by a loud hissing which I first thought was him farting. When the balloon's ascent started to slow I knew that flatulence wasn't the issue this time. The craft's envelope had been punctured somewhere above us.

'Now what do we do?' asked Jack, a not-unreasonable question in the circumstances.

'Plan B,' replied Miss Muffet, reaching into the same wicker box she'd removed the crossbow from and lifting out a smaller, wide box.

'What's that?' I foolishly enquired.

'I'm glad you asked, Harry,' she said, handing the box to me. 'It's a puncture repair kit and you're going to have to be the one doing the repairing. I'll have to try to keep the rest of those birds away while attempting to stop us from crashing at the same time. There's no one else who can do it.'

I looked at my two accomplices. She was right: Jack was too young to risk doing something so dangerous and Basili was just too fat. It was me or certain death – or possibly certain death for me and survival for the others. 'What exactly do I have to do?' I asked, not that I really wanted to know the answer.

The Curds and Whey Mystery

Miss Muffet pointed up at the huge mass of the balloon's envelope above. 'You'll need to climb up on the outside of that, find the hole and repair it as fast as you can. The envelope is surrounded by netting so you'll have something to hold on to.'

This was sounding worse by the minute. 'Outside, as in outside?'

'Afraid so, and you'd better be quick; we're losing altitude.'

The balloon's envelope was already starting to sag where it had been punctured and, of course, the birds hadn't been so considerate as to pierce it near the basket. Oh, no, they'd gone for maximum effect by making the hole near the top, right where it was at its most inaccessible.

'Harry.' The urgency in Miss Muffet's voice brought me back to a reality I didn't want to know about.

'All right, all right, I'm going.' I grabbed one of the steel supports that secured the basket to the burner and hauled myself up onto its edge. It was then I realised just how high we actually were. The entirety of Grimmtown sprawled below and tiny clouds drifted by. Beside me, the huge mass of the beanstalk twisted and turned as it stretched away from us towards a large cloud mass above.

'This isn't a good idea,' I muttered as I pulled myself upright and balanced on the basket.

'Here you are, Mr Harry,' said Basili from below. 'Perhaps you are tying this to yourself in the event that you are falling.' He reached up and tied some rope around my waist.

'Thanks, Basili,' I said. 'Whatever you do, don't let go.'

'You are depending on me,' Basili replied proudly. However one interpreted that sentence, it was correct in every respect.

I pulled on the rope to make sure it was secure then, taking a deep breath that was part terror, part resignation and part I'm-probably-going-to-die-now, I took firm hold of the netting around the envelope and began my very careful ascent of the balloon.

Initially, it wasn't too bad. I was able to work my way upwards by grabbing the next strand of netting above me, digging in with my trotters and pushing myself up. Just when I was about to shout down to the others that this wasn't too difficult, I reached the spot where the balloon's surface bulged outwards and quickly corrected myself as I began to edge out, my body hanging parallel to the ground far below, clinging on for dear life.

Inch by desperate inch, I crawled along the balloon's surface making sure each next grip was secure before letting go the previous one. Slowly, I made my way around the curve until I had passed the equator and was lying on the envelope once more. Above me, I could see where the bird had punctured the surface. I focused on that spot and tried not to look down as it got closer and closer.

The Curds and Whey Mystery

I was concentrating so much on the hole in the balloon that I almost didn't notice the birds dive-bombing me. Sensing what I was trying to do they launched an all-out attack to try to knock me off the netting, but I saw their approach at the last minute and waved my arms furiously – which almost had the desired effect as I lost my balance and swung away from the balloon, only grabbing on at the last second.

Above, the birds screeched their frustration and were preparing for a second assault when one of them dropped out of the sky in a flurry of feathers. Miss Muffet had hit the target once more.

That gave the rest of the flock something to think about as they circled the balloon warily, waiting for the chance to have another go at me. At the same time I was gradually getting nearer the puncture, pushing my way along the envelope step by very careful step.

At last I reached my destination. The hole didn't look too big and I didn't anticipate any difficulty in fixing it. Removing the repair kit from my pocket, I opened it and took out a large tube of glue. I quickly applied it to the area around the puncture before cutting off a strip of material from the roll provided and using it to cover the hole. Easy, just like repairing a bicycle wheel – except bicycles tended not to develop punctures while thousands of feet in the air with the wind whistling around the repairer, threatening to blow him into oblivion.

I was patting down the patch, making sure it was secure, when I heard a shout from below. 'They've punctured the far side of the balloon. Quick, Harry, get going.'

And so it went on. I'd no sooner repair one hole than another would appear somewhere else on the balloon, despite Miss Muffet's best efforts to keep the birds at bay. I travelled around the surface of the balloon, doing repair after repair, conscious of the fact that I was running out of both glue and patches, when I heard the phrase I never thought I'd hear spoken again.

'It's okay, Harry, I think we're here.'

I finally took the time to look around. I'd been so caught up in my role as a porcine puncture repair kit that I hadn't realised how high we now were. The balloon was nestling snugly against the beanstalk just below a huge mass of grey cloud that stretched in all directions. Typically, just when I thought we were safe, the birds made one last attack – this time on me. The flock of feathered fiends flapped around my head, pecking and clawing. In panic, I tried to swat them with both arms, forgetting for a second where exactly I was. Losing my balance I slid down the balloon's surface so fast I was unable to grab onto the netting while the birds squawked triumphantly – and possibly even mockingly – as I fell. With a howl of terror I plummeted off the balloon, seeing the concerned passengers in the basket pass me by in a blur. Anticipating a long and painful fall, I covered my head with my arms – not that it would make much difference really.

Fortunately, Basili's knot held and I came to an abrupt halt, swinging gently from side to side, looking up at the basket as three heads peered over the edge and down at me.

'Mr Harry, you are being okay, yes?' asked a concerned Basili.

'I'm fine,' I replied as they hauled me up. 'But the next time, I think we'll climb.'

14

Cloud Kingdom

Happy that we were temporarily safe, Miss Muffet threw out a small anchor that bit into the trunk of the beanstalk and secured the balloon.

'Okay, gentlemen, we climb from here. It's not too far to the cloud, so keep quiet and try not to be seen. As soon as the beanstalk broke the cloud-cover, chances are the giants set up a temporary border control to manage any visitors, so we'll have to get by them first.' She climbed out of the basket and held it steady. 'Everyone out.'

Jack hopped nimbly out of the balloon, followed ,somewhat less agilely, by Basili who had to receive some help from me (which basically meant me standing under him and, with much huffing and puffing, pushing him over the edge). Seconds later I stood on a large leafy branch beside the others. Above us the cloud-cover blocked out the sun, forcing us to finish our ascent in semi-darkness.

'The branches are wide enough so you shouldn't be in any danger,' Miss Muffet advised. 'Just be careful and you'll be fine.'

Slowly we climbed through the foliage towards the fluffy mass above. 'I thought clouds are just made of water,' I whispered to Miss Muffet. 'What's going to stop us from sinking through them once we get there?'

'The giants have magic powers and one of the basic ones makes the clouds solid. It only works on those clouds they live on, though; otherwise they'd play havoc with air traffic control.'

She had a point.

'So now what?' I asked as we reached the point where beanstalk and cloud met.

'Let me take a peek and we'll see.' Cautiously, Miss Muffet poked her head up through the clouds, took a look and quickly pulled her head back down. 'Just as I thought,' she whispered. 'There's a heavily guarded immigration post covering all access from the beanstalk. They look pretty mean and are keeping a very close watch. We're going to have to come up with some sort of distraction.'

'What kind of guards are they?' Our success rate at distracting them very much depended on their level of stupidity. In my experience it ranged from mildly dull (ogres) to extremely thick (gnomes) with degrees of dimness in between.

'Not sure. I think they were goblins.' Miss Muffet said after thinking about it for a moment.

'Well, that's good.' It was too. Goblins featured just above gnomes on the stupidity scale. Any half-decent distraction would probably work on them. Obviously they were the best the giant could muster at such short notice.

'And speaking of distractions.' She looked at me and, from the expression on her face, I just knew that whatever diversion she had in mind would somehow involve me. 'You're going to have to go up there.'

'Why me?' I said. 'Haven't I been through enough already?'

'Yes, but you're the smooth talker. If anyone can distract them it's you.'

'Fine, whatever you say,' I replied. There didn't seem to be any alternative.

Bracing myself to strut my stuff, I looked up at the clouds once more. 'I have another question,' I said.

Miss Muffet rolled her eyes. 'This really isn't the time, Harry; we've got other things to worry about.'

'I know but, if the clouds are supposed to be solid, how did you manage to stick your head up through them? What's stopping me from banging mine when I go up there?'

'They're magic clouds, Harry; they allow access up through them but are solid for everyone on the surface. How else would the beanstalks get through?'

A few minutes later, a bit dishevelled and only slightly presentable, I poked my head up through the clouds and shouted at the goblins, 'Oi, you lot, my craft has broken down and I need some help.' Pulling myself up to cloud level, I reached into my coat, grabbed my wallet and waved it at them. 'I've got money.'

At the immigration post, all four goblins took a look at me (or maybe it was my wallet) and, as one, they rushed to my assistance. As the first two arrived I grabbed them and, before they could react, banged their heads together. As they collapsed on the ground I threw myself at the other two, who had stopped in confusion as their colleagues fell (see, thick, like I said). There was a satisfying crunch as I crushed them beneath me and, moments later, with my team's help all were securely bound and gagged and dropped into the basket of the balloon below so they'd be out of sight.

'You'd have thought that if they were that concerned with security, giants would have a brighter militia than goblins,' I said, as the last one disappeared from view.

'I suspect they were a short-term solution because the beanstalk appeared so suddenly. Normally, immigration is a lot tighter,' Miss Muffet said.

'If you don't mind my saying so, you seem very well versed in this whole area,' I said to her.

'It was my father,' she replied. 'He used to sit me on his knee and tell me about his adventures. He spent a lot of time in places like this. Anyway, it's the kind of thing you need to know when you run a B&B. Guests are always asking how to visit.'

Now that we'd successfully – if somewhat illegally – crossed the border, I finally had a chance to look around. In the distance, the skyline was dominated by an enormous castle. It was so huge it made Aladdin's look like a hut. Towers stretched upwards, gigantic walls encircled the castle's base and the moat that surrounded it was the size of a large river.

'So this giant's a big fellow then?' I said, looking apprehensively at the massive edifice.

'Neringus? Yes, he's one of the biggest, I believe. Rumour has it he's about seventy feet tall. That's the thing about giants, they're giants.'

'Seventy feet?' I was gobsmacked. 'That's big, even for a giant.'

'That's because he's managed to live to be over three hundred. Most giants don't get to survive that long. There are too many adventurers just waiting to have a go. Giants spend their lives constantly looking over their shoulders, waiting for the next hero to try to steal their golden goose or magic harp. This guy's one of the greats.'

'And what about Licken and Lurkey, are they in league with him?' If they were it would be quite an achievement. I still wasn't sure how they'd managed to pull it off. Not only had they managed to infest Miss Muffet's with spiders but they'd stolen the magic bean and made a beeline for Neringus's kingdom without any fear for their lives. Mind you, I still wasn't convinced. They just weren't that imaginative.

'I shouldn't think so,' Miss Muffet said. 'Remember they didn't know the treasure was here either until a short while ago. There's no way they could have planned this. Still,' she looked around carefully, 'there's no sign of them here. Unless they had something to bargain with, they'd have ended up on a spit, being the goblins' dinner, once they popped their heads above the clouds. Goblins are quite partial to poultry.'

I considered what Queenie had said. 'That's what worries me. Neither of them is too bright, or so I thought, and I've known them for years. They're not smart enough to pull something like this off. They must be getting help.'

'From who?' asked Miss Muffet.

'One of the other guests,' I said. 'I'm still not sure which one, though I have my suspicions' – which included most of them right about now.

Other than the castle, there wasn't much to see. Gigantic trees dotted the landscape like green skyscrapers and the only obvious road (and it was very obvious as it was about a mile wide) bisected the cloud and led straight to the castle. There were no villages (the giant had probably eaten all the villagers) and no other signs of life. All told, it was a pretty desolate place.

I pointed to the castle. 'Well, it looks like we're walking.' In fact, after having worn heels for a day, I found I was able to manage the cloud's grey, spongy surface without any difficulty. The others weaved from side to side, having trouble maintaining their balance. It would be a while until they found their cloud-legs.

Together we made our way along the road towards the architectural monstrosity ahead. As we walked, I tried to formulate a plan. What would we find in the castle? Would Licken and Lurkey be waiting with the giant, ready to make a meal of us (literally and metaphorically), or would we manage to find the treasure and get it back to sea level? As the fowl duo was dumber than a bucket of gerbils, someone had to be helping them; but who? Questions, questions – and not an answer in sight.

Then a far more important thought struck me: we were walking towards a large castle, occupied by a very unpleasant giant and, other than the occasional tree, there was no obvious cover to stop us being seen by any lookouts. We were sitting ducks, so to speak.

'Well, to be honest we don't have much choice,' Miss Muffet pointed out when I mentioned it. 'We could try to disguise ourselves as goblins, but it would mean climbing back down to the balloon to undress them and I really don't think there's any chance their outfits would fit us.' She looked pointedly at Basili and me.

'So, what do we do?' Jack asked. 'I don't want to end up being eaten.'

'I don't either, Jack, but maybe we can use the trees as cover.' As plans went, it wasn't up to much owing to the scarcity of actual vegetation, but at least it was a suggestion – albeit a relatively useless one.

'Perhaps we are being continuing with the film plan.' Basili had been quiet up to now and when he said that I wished he'd stayed quiet.

'That's the most—' I began, before being interrupted by Miss Muffet.

'The most brilliant suggestion I've heard,' she said. Clearly she didn't hear much by way of brilliant suggestions in the course of running a B&B.

'No, listen,' she continued. 'Why not try it? What have we got to lose?'

'Our heads for one thing,' I pointed out. 'We're here illegally; Licken and Lurkey know who we are; and do I need to point out that a giant, with a healthy appetite for meat and who isn't too fussy about what type, lives here?'

'And I suppose you have a better idea?' Miss Muffet said.

'Well, there's always the old standby,' I said. She raised an enquiring eyebrow. 'Wait until dark.'

Miss Muffet was about to say something, clearly thought the better of it when she realised she had no other suggestions and wisely chose to remain silent.

'There, that's settled then. Now let's find somewhere to shelter.' I headed towards the nearest tree and sat down against the trunk. Branches that were so big they could have made a successful living as trees in Grimmtown overhung our location and provided the perfect cover. As long as we stayed here, we'd never be seen from the castle.

Beside me, Jack looked up through the leaf cover at the sky as he huddled against Basili for warmth. 'Well, at least it's not ra...' He had just opened his mouth when there was a loud clap of thunder and the skies above, clearly intent on inflicting as much misery as possible on us, unleashed a deluge that could only loosely have been described as rain, such was its intensity. Although the tree provided great cover from prying eyes, as shelter it left much to be desired. Torrents of water flowed down leaves the size of umbrellas and submerged us in a cascade of freezing rain.

'Thanks, Jack,' I said, as water streamed down my face, ruining what was left of my make-up.

'Don't mention it,' he said miserably as he tried to shelter under Basili's jacket.

'Look on the bright side.' Miss Muffet stood up and tried to wring out her hair (it didn't make much difference). 'With rain this heavy, the guards won't be too keen on keeping watch and it'll provide decent enough cover. And we can't get any wetter now, can we?'

'I suppose not. Okay, gang, let's walk.' I stood up, watched water flow off me in mini-streams and squelched forwards towards the castle. Grumbling loudly, Basili followed with Miss Muffet and Jack bringing up the rear.

Miss Muffet was right about one thing: the rain certainly provided enough cover. It pummelled us relentlessly as we walked, cascading down around us and soaking us through. It was like being underwater. At least there was one benefit: no one was interested in talking much. We trudged on, wrapped in our own silent miseries, hoping all the while that the castle was getting nearer – we certainly couldn't see it through the deluge, large though it may have been.

I don't know how long we walked for. It could have been minutes, it could have been hours. Time seemed to pass differently under the incessant downpour. All I knew was that, out of nowhere the road ended and I was suddenly walking on wood. I held out my arms to block the others. 'Everyone, stop right now. I think we're there.'

Ahead I could just make out a large dark space which I imagined was the castle entrance. That meant that we were now standing on the huge drawbridge that extended over the moat. From what I could make out, the entrance seemed to be unguarded. Was it going to be that easy? Just to be sure, I indicated to the others to stay where they were and crept forward for a closer look. Once I was under the huge arch at the far end of the drawbridge, I was sheltered from the rain, for which I gave a silent prayer of thanks. Ahead of me, the arch opened out into a huge covered lobby with doors in all the walls and a gigantic staircase leading to the upper levels. On the far side of the arch, almost hidden from view, was a guard post. Sensibly, if somewhat against orders, the guards had obviously elected to perform their duties from inside the comfort and warmth of their hut. In other circumstances I may have been appalled by their cavalier attitude to their work; today I was mostly grateful. Just to be sure, I sneaked over to the hut, crouched under the window and very cautiously took a look in. It seemed, from what I could observe, that the security goblins' idea of keeping watch amounted to huddling around a table, playing cards and accusing each other of cheating.

I crept back to the others and advised them of the situation. 'If we're very quiet we should make it past that hut without any difficulty. After that, as I don't know where we're going, I suggest we head for the nearest door and then decide what to do next.' My plan was greeted by a round of ragged and less than enthusiastic nods.

Single file and crouched down, we sneaked past the guard hut, along the wall towards the first door. When we got there I realised we had a problem.

'Anyone got any ideas how to reach that?' I looked up at the door handle. It was the perfect height for a giant, but, some thirty-five feet above us, it was more than a little inaccessible.

'Well, if we had some rope we could make a lasso and pull it down,' Jack suggested.

'Rope anyone?' I asked, to be greeted by much shaking of heads. 'Okay then, it looks like we'll have to invoke Plan B.'

'Plan B?' Basili said. 'What is Plan B?'

'Something that you'll play a vital role in.' I waved him forward. 'Stand there.'

Basili did as instructed. 'Now, I'm going to climb up on your shoulders.' This was a lot more difficult than it sounded. We were all so wet, every time I attempted to clamber up on Basili's back, I slid back down again.

Miss Muffet was becoming exasperated. 'The longer we hang around here the more likely it is that one of those guards will come out for a quick smoke or the giant will decide to go for his evening constitutional. We'll be pretty defenceless then, balanced one on top of the other, won't we?'

Her powers of persuasion were very effective. The thought of the castle's owner finding us gave my mountaineering skills a temporary boost and seconds later I was balancing precariously on Basili's ample shoulders and extending my hand down to Miss Muffet.

I hoisted her onto my shoulders. She teetered back and forth for a second, but, thankfully, regained her balance before she could bring the whole tower down.

'How far to the handle?' I asked.

'It's still out of reach,' Miss Muffet said. 'Once Jack is up here, he might be able to grab it.'

I looked down at Jack who was waiting expectantly down below. 'You're up.'

He must have had monkey ancestors as he shinned up all three of us and balanced on Miss Muffet's shoulders like he was going up stairs.

'Can you reach it?' I asked.

'Maybe, if I jump,' Jack shouted down from above. 'But it's very big. I can't pull it down. I'll have to hang off it. Just a sec.' There was a brief pause, then he said, 'It's on its way.' Followed seconds later by, 'Oh, no.'

Oh no? Why the 'oh no'? 'Jack, what's going on?' As I spoke the door opened inwards and our tower collapsed onto the (fortunately) soft carpet inside. Other than a few bumps where we landed on each other, everyone seemed okay. I did a quick headcount. Basili was lying under me, pushing me off. Miss Muffet sat on the ground rubbing her back. And Jack – where was Jack?

'Help,' came a voice from above. 'Someone help me.' Jack was still dangling from the handle. 'I can't hold on much longer.'

'Quick,' I said to the others. 'We need to find something to break his fall.' Anxiously the three of us looked around the huge room. Furniture the size of houses towered above us; the carpet stretched off to walls that seemed miles away. There didn't seem to be anything that we could use.

'There, look.' Miss Muffet pointed at a small white bundle partially hidden by a chair leg. She ran over and pulled at it. 'Perfect.'

We followed her over and looked at what she'd found.

'Why is there a sheet on the floor?' Basili asked as he helped her pull it across the room.

'I don't think it's a sheet; I think it's a handkerchief.' Miss Muffet panted as she heaved the mass of cloth along the carpet.

I grabbed the other end and helped. 'I hope it's clean,' I said.

'Don't even go there,' Miss Muffet said through gritted teeth. 'That's the least of our worries right now.'

When we'd reached the door, Miss Muffet and I grabbed a corner, Basili seized the opposite edge and we stretched out what I now saw was a clean hanky.

'Everyone hold on tight,' I ordered and looked up at the small figure dangling above us. 'Jack, let go the handle. We'll catch you.'

Either he was very trusting or he couldn't hold on any longer. I had barely finished speaking when he dropped into the taut hanky, bounced up once and landed in the middle again.

'Wow, that was fun,' he said, poking his head out of the tangle of cloth.

I checked him for any injuries, but he seemed none the worse for his experience. 'Are you okay?'

'Yep,' he said. 'What's the plan?'

Before I could reply, there was the sound of applause from the far side of the room and a female voice said, 'Marvellous, absolutely marvellous. Can you do it again?'

15

Fee, Fie, Foe, Something-or-Other

The only thing I was sure of as I swung around to see who had spoken was that it almost certainly wasn't the giant. If he'd been in the room he could hardly have missed our amateur acrobatics and rescue stunt – and we'd probably have noticed him by now anyway. That didn't mean we weren't in danger, though: chances were, anyone living in the giant's castle probably wouldn't be friendly.

'Okay everyone, be on your guard,' I whispered. 'See if you can spot who's doing the talking.'

Miss Muffet pointed. 'I think it came from over there, somewhere near all those musical instruments.'

'How incredibly observant of you,' said the voice once more. This time it sounded as if it was taunting us. 'Maybe you should take a closer look.'

Huddled together, we crept carefully across the wide expanse of carpet, towards the array of instruments Miss Muffet had pointed out.

'I am opinioning that we are being in the music room,' whispered Basili.

'You think?' I said. 'What was your first clue?'

'Quiet, the pair of you,' Miss Muffet hissed. 'This isn't the time or the place.'

'I'd listen to the lady,' said the mysterious voice once more. 'She knows what she's talking about.'

Miss Muffet turned towards me. 'I think it's coming from behind that harp.'

'Oh, you're so warm. Have another guess.' Now the voice was starting to irritate me.

I looked over towards the instruments. A huge, definitely giant-sized wooden harp towered above us. The instrument's front column had been carved into the shape of a woman in long flowing robes, arms clasped above her head. The harp was a bit worse for wear. Long, deep scratches ran the length of the column and it looked as though chunks of wood had recently been cut out of the base. It had clearly seen better days. A stool – presumably for the absent harpist – sat to one side. If there was someone hiding behind the harp, I couldn't see them. All I could make out was a collection of other instruments, all on display stands. Cellos, violins and basses stood to one side, brasses dominated the centre and a large grand piano took up the left-hand side of the display area.

I nudged Miss Muffet. 'Are you sure you heard the voice from behind the harp? I can't see anything.'

The carved woman on the harp turned her head and looked down at us. 'That's because it is the harp, you dunderhead,' she said, her voice dripping sarcasm. She unclasped her arms and positioned them on her hips. 'You're not too bright, are you?' She took a closer look at me. 'And are you wearing make-up?'

'Take it from me, you're not seeing us at our best,' I said wearily.

'That much is certain,' Basili added.

'More to the point,' I interrupted, before the conversation went further off the rails. 'Who exactly are you?'

'Why, I'm the famous magic harp.' The harp drew herself up to full height. 'Of course, you've heard of me.' It was more a statement than a question.

'The harp that Jack the Giantkiller stole?' There seemed to be a lot of Jacks cropping up in this particular case.

'No, no, no!' The harp's face twisted angrily. 'Do you honestly think anyone would be capable of stealing me? I'm not exactly convenient to carry, am I?' She had a point. From where I stood she looked very heavy indeed. I imagined it would take a small team of men and an industrial crane to move her.

'So what did he...'

The harp interrupted as if anticipating my question. 'He stole a lyre okay, L-Y-R-E. Not a harp, a lyre – and a pretty cheap one at that.' She shook her head. 'Giantkillers: thick as soup. It's not as if it's easy to confuse us.'

Once more the conversation was threatening to derail and plunge into a canyon of digressions.

'Look Miss Harp, Harpy or whatever your name is. We're looking for a chicken and a turkey that might have arrived here earlier today. Have you seen them?'

The harp smirked. 'And I thought giantkillers were stupid. Those two make most other adventurers look like geniuses.'

'So they were here then?' I asked.

'Oh yeah, they were here. They even whispered about trying to steal me, until I warned them off. I told them I'd tell Neringus what they were at. That sorted them out. But before they ran off they did this.' She pointed to the scratches and damage to the harp's base. 'Vandals. I'm going to need some repair work and a new coat of varnish because of them.'

'And where are they now?'

'Oh, they headed off with my master. Knowing him, I expect they're chicken soup by now.'

I didn't think so; they were here for a reason and I suspected the giant was tied up in it. It was possible they'd be dinner eventually, just not yet. 'Where did he take them?'

The Curds and Whey Mystery

'His study is on the first floor. Top of the landing, turn left, first door.' The harp smirked. 'Will you be doing your team pyramid act to get up the stairs? If you are, can you leave the door open, I'd love to watch.'

Now that presented a problem. We'd had enough trouble just opening the door to the music room; getting up a flight of stairs presented a challenge an order of magnitude more difficult – and we had to do it without being seen.

'Anyone got any suggestions?' I asked the others. Silence greeted my question. Team Harry clearly weren't on the ball right about now. 'Anyone?'

'I think you might not need to climb the stairs after all,' the harp interrupted. 'If I'm not mistaken the owner of the house is on his way down.'

'What? The giant is on his way? We need to hide. Now!'

From outside the door came the noise of something very large and very heavy descending the stairs. I looked around in panic. Other than the furniture there wasn't much by way of hiding places. Maybe we could take cover behind a table leg and hope we weren't seen. It was a long shot, but it was the only option we had.

'Everyone, get to the table,' I shouted and ran towards the towering wooden structure. Basili crouched beside me. The other two had taken cover behind the large percussion section. I looked at the harp. 'And if you say a word or do anything to attract attention, I'll carve my initials into your pretty wooden head. Are we clear?'

The harp gulped once and nodded. 'I already need some restoration work; I don't fancy needing more.'

There was a loud crashing from above as the giant pushed the door fully open and entered the room. I felt the floor vibrate as he walked across the room and paused beside our hiding place. Peeping out, I could see a gigantic boot and the bottom of Neringus's trousers. Slowly, he bent down towards me. How had he seen us?

I was caught between cowering where I was and making a futile attempt to run for the door when a loud voice proclaimed, 'FEE, FIE, FOE, FU—, oh there it is,' and the giant picked up the handkerchief we'd used to rescue Jack moments earlier. As the giant turned to leave the room he paused once more and I heard him sniff loudly. 'FEE, FIE. FOE, FUM, I SMELL THE BLOOD OF AN...well, I'm not exactly sure, but I do smell something. Unless I'm mistaken, we have intruders. How inconvenient. I shall have to talk to those goblins. They seem to be less than efficient.' He began to prowl around the room, sniffing constantly, trying to pinpoint our location.

'Sire, if I may.' The treacherous harp pointed at the table. 'I think you'll find what you're looking for behind that table leg there.' Before Basili or I could run, the giant reached down, picked us up in each hand and dangled us in front of him. 'Now, what have we here, hmmm?' He scrutinized us carefully, turning us around and examining us from all sides. 'How unusual: a most unattractive male of the pig species and a large gentleman with a faint echo of magic. I suspect you have quite an interesting story to tell and I do so look forward to hearing it before dinner.' He smiled. 'Then again, as you probably will be dinner, I expect that you'll be finished telling it long before that.'

As the giant took us from the room, I managed to grab Miss Muffet's attention, waving at her to stay hidden until we left the room. I couldn't say whether she got the message before the door was slammed behind us and, firmly in the giant's clutches, we ascended the stairs.

16

The Not-So-Great Escape

S uspended fifty feet above the ground, we were carried along a landing and into the giant's study. He walked towards a huge desk and sat down, dropping me and Basili into a glass bowl under a reading lamp. As he studied us, I took the opportunity to take a closer look at him too. Long brown hair hung down around his shoulders, green eyes stared at us in fascination and his nose bore evidence of more than one confrontation (though whether with other giants or human adventurers, I couldn't say). Judging by the frilly shirt, puffed at the sleeves, I was getting a definite New Romantic vibe from him. His smile wasn't especially friendly, not that I expected it would be. As a rule, anyone with a penchant for eating his visitors probably wasn't the friendly type.

'Well now then, and who do we have here, hmmm?' Even when he spoke quietly it was like standing beside a jet engine as it prepared to take off. I covered my ears to deaden the sound – it didn't make much difference.

I decided that, as it had worked reasonably well up to now, I'd go for the film crew ruse once more; well, we still sort of looked the part, although perhaps a little more dishevelled than I might have liked. 'I'm Harry du Crêpe, personal assistant to Alain Schmidt-Heye, world renowned film director. This is he.' I waved at a terrified Basili who was cowering beside me. 'Snap out of it,' I hissed at him while kicking him none too gently on the ankle. 'Our lives depend on this.'

Neringus's smile stretched even wider. He seemed to be very amused at us. 'Movies, eh? How nice. Are you sure you're not perhaps Harry Pigg and his assistant Basili, the former genie, hmmm?'

Busted!

I looked up at Neringus, 'Licken and Lurkey?'

The giant rubbed his stomach and belched loudly. It was like being caught in an unpleasant-smelling wind tunnel. 'Indeed, the feathered fowl duo. I must confess, I am so looking forward to having them for dinner. I'm feeling a tad unwell and I'm told that chicken soup does wonders for a cold.'

'You're going to eat them?'

'But of course; they were trespassing, as, I must point out, are you.' Now that wasn't something I wanted to hear. It wasn't that I was overly concerned as to their fate; I was more concerned that we were likely to meet the same end. 'In fact, why don't you wave to them; they're over there.' He pointed to a shelf on the far wall. Sitting in a covered bowl the size of a truck, very like the one we were in, only much bigger, were a very unhappy-looking Licken and Lurkey. They gave me an abashed wave. I didn't return it.

'So now what?' I asked the giant.

'Now? Why you're going to be dinner, like I've already told you. Why? Did you have something else in mind?'

To be honest, all thoughts of solving the case had vanished once Neringus had mentioned we were on the menu. The only thing on my mind now was trying to escape, initially from the bowl and eventually from Neringus's kingdom. I wasn't sure right now which was going to be tougher.

Neringus stood up and walked towards the door. 'Don't go anywhere now. I'll be expecting you to be here when I get back.' He smirked as he left the room. I was starting to dislike him deeply.

Once he was gone I turned to Basili. 'All right, let's get out of here,' I said. 'It shouldn't be too hard.' When I tried to clamber up the walls of the bowl I found out just how difficult it was going to be. Trotters and glass were not a good combination. No matter how hard I tried, I couldn't get any purchase on the surface and kept sliding back down. Even if we tried a cut-down variation on our human pyramid of earlier, we still weren't tall enough to reach the bowl's rim.

Every attempt either resulted in another slide down the glass or me collapsing in a heap on top of poor Basili.

'Oh, Mr Harry,' he moaned after our latest attempt had ended in failure. 'I am not wanting to be a giant's evening meal. What are we to do?'

'I'm thinking, Basili. I'm thinking.' Which was true. I just wasn't coming up with anything remotely resembling an escape plan. As I lay at the bottom of the bowl, out of the corner of my eye I caught something moving: Licken and Lurkey were waving frantically at me. As they were partly responsible for me being in this mess, I chose to ignore them, but it wasn't to be. Basili nudged me in the ribs.

'Mr Harry, I think they are trying most hard to communicate with us.'

'How? Semaphore? Morse Code? Interpretive Dance?' I really wasn't interested.

'No, Mr Harry, they are writing something.'

'Writing? On what?' I still wasn't interested.

'On the glass.'

I suspected there wasn't anything that Licken and Lurkey might say that could possibly interest me, but I took a quick look. Their first attempt at communication seemed to confirm this. Using what I suspected was something out of his make-up pouch, Licken had written: 'DON'T CLIME GLAS WE TRIED THAT TO IT DUZENT WORK.'

Well, that really encouraged me. We were trapped in glass bowls in a giant's stronghold and all they seemed to be interested in was stating the blindingly obvious. Well, we weren't going to get much help from that direction. I urged Basili to ignore them. 'Unfortunately, they won't go away, but we can look in the other direction.'

'But Mr Neringus will be eating them,' he wailed.

'Better them than us,' I replied.

'Oh, Mr Harry, that is being very cruel.' Basili slumped down beside me. 'Look, they are being writing another message.'

'Let me guess: "we're all going to die," just spelled very badly.'

'No, it is something about a trezzar. What is a trezzar?'

'Trezzar?' I looked over at the other bowl. 'WE NO WHERE TREZZAR IS.'

'I don't know anyone called Trezzar,' I said to Basili. 'Do you?'

'I am not aware of anyone with that name,' he replied after thinking for a moment.

'So what are they try...?' Then it struck me. 'It's not a who, it's a what. They know where the badly spelled treasure is. They've found Sinbad's fortune.' Then an even worse thought struck me. 'If we get out of here, that means we'll now have to rescue them, too.'

'But, of course, that is meaning that we must be getting ourselves out of here first,' Basili pointed out, taking his 'stating the transparently obvious' cue from the other two.

'Well, that's true,' I replied. 'But I confidently expect that we'll be out of this bowl imminently.'

'You are having a plan?' Basili jumped up and down in excitement and it wasn't a pretty sight.

'I'm not.' Basili's face dropped once more. 'But I suspect they are,' and I pointed up to the huge anglepoise lamp that overhung the bowl. Perched on top, lowering a rope, were Miss Muffet and Jack. The cavalry were here.

'Good work, guys,' I shouted as the rope descended.

'Sorry it took so long,' Miss Muffet replied. 'The stairs were a bit tricky.'

'Yeah,' Jack piped in. 'I'd have been here quicker only for her.'

Miss Muffet rolled her eyes and wisely chose to ignore him.

'I'm glad you're here now,' I said as I grabbed the rope – which was actually a piece of giantish string – and clambered up the side of the bowl.

Basili wasn't as limber as I, so it took a more concerted effort to get him out, all three of us dragging the rope upwards while he dangled uselessly. Eventually, he was able to grab the rim and pull himself up onto it. 'Now what?' he asked.

'We lower you onto the desk then I follow you down.' More grunting, groaning and near-misses ensued until the ex-genie was, finally, safely on the giant writing pad that the bowl rested on. Once he was safe, I shinned down after him and waited for Miss Muffet and Jack to join us.

'Okay,' Miss Muffet said, 'let's get out of here.' She stopped when she saw the expression on my face. 'Uh oh, I suspect that doesn't mean good news is about to follow.'

I pointed at Lurkey and Licken. 'We need to get them out too; they know where the loot is.'

Miss Muffet stamped her foot on the desk. 'Dammit, there's always something.' She looked across at the bowl. Although it was only at the far side of the study and a short walk by giant standards, to us it would be like negotiating an assault course. 'Do we have to?'

'I'm afraid so,' I said. 'Without them we're stuck. Mind you, I don't know how we're going to get over there.'

Miss Muffet scanned the desk. 'Maybe we don't have to.'

I raised an enquiring eyebrow.

'Look, it could take us the rest of the day just to get up to that shelf and, after that, we'd still have to get them out of the bowl.'

I nodded for her to continue.

'What if we could just break the bowl from here?' She ran over to the side of the desk and forced open a large paper box. 'Ah, just what I was looking for.' She reached into the box and hauled out a long rubber band. 'Here, give me a hand to take these out.'

The rest of us looked blankly at her.

'Now, please,' and her tone of voice suggested that arguing with her would not be a good idea.

'You heard the lady,' I said to the others. 'Let's go.' Together we dragged a number of rubber bands from the box and formed them into a big pile on the desk.

'Right, now we tie them together – and make sure they're proper knots. I don't want them coming loose at a crucial moment.'

'Care to elaborate on the plan?' I asked, mystified.

'In a moment; just keep tying.' She ran to the far side of the desk. 'I'll be back shortly; I just need to find something.'

Jack looked at me. 'Harry, what's she doing?'

'Your guess is as good as mine,' I said to him, 'but she seems to know what she's at.'

By the time Miss Muffet came back, carrying a large stone, we'd tied the rubber bands into a long strand. 'Paperweight,' she announced and looked at our work appreciatively. 'Not bad, boys; not bad at all.' She grabbed one end of the strand. 'Now if we tie this to here,' she muttered as she wrapped it around the stem of the lamp, 'and this end to...' She looked around the surface of the desk. 'Ah, good; this will do nicely.' Taking the other end of the rope of rubber bands, she secured it to a giant marble pen holder. Once both ends were tied off she grabbed the middle of what had become an improvised catapult and hauled it back. As the bands began to stretch, she struggled to keep it taut.

'Harry. Genie. Help me.'

The two of us stood beside her and took the strain. Together we pulled the rubber rope further back until our muscles were straining to keep the tension on it.

'I don't think we can hold this much longer,' I grunted.

'Jack,' Miss Muffet shouted. 'Grab the stone and put it on the rubber band – and hurry.'

Jack scurried around to where Miss Muffet had dropped the stone and rolled it over to where we stood. 'It's very heavy,' he said.

'I know, Jack, but just try your best, okay.' I could hear the tension in her voice. She wouldn't be able to hold on much longer.

Jack put his arms under the stone and slowly began to lift.

'That's it,' Miss Muffet encouraged him. 'Just a little bit more. You're almost there.'

Inch by painful inch, Jack raised the stone until it was level with Miss Muffet's arms.

'Now, drop it on the elastic band on top of my forearms and stand well back. We'll only get one shot at this.'

Jack eased the stone onto the rubber band as instructed. 'Stand well back, Jack,' she ordered. 'On the count of three, everyone let go; one, two, three.'

To be honest, I wasn't able to hold on any longer anyway. As soon as she said 'three' I let go and watched as the stone flew across the room towards Licken and Lurkey's bowl. It was obvious almost as soon as it was fired that it was going to miss by some distance.

'Dammit,' Miss Muffet shouted. 'I thought I'd aimed it correctly.'

'Don't be hard on yourself,' I said to her. 'It was a one in a million cha...'

'And one that might just pay off,' Jack interrupted. 'Look.'

We followed the stone as it sailed through the air. Although it missed the bowl by the proverbial country mile, it cannoned off a picture frame on the shelf above, deflected sideways and smacked into a vase that sat on the edge of the shelf. The vase teetered from side to side before falling off the shelf and bouncing onto the bowl on the shelf below as it plummeted to its destruction on the floor. There was a loud crash and the bowl began to break. We watched in fascination as the glass cracked and shattered around Licken and Lurkey. Fortunately (or unfortunately, depending on your point of view), neither of them seemed to have been injured in the process.

Miss Muffet turned to us proudly. 'Of course, I meant it all the time.' She looked at our disbelieving faces. 'Yes, really.'

But she didn't get too much opportunity to bask in her glory.

'Um, Mr Harry, I am believing that the bird people are leaving us behind.'

'See ya, suckers.' Free at last, Licken and Lurkey were using their wings to glide to the floor. I certainly wouldn't have called it flying.

The Curds and Whey Mystery

Miss Muffet looked on as the pair of them reached the ground safely and scuttled out the door, giving us a quick wave as they did so. 'There's gratitude for you,' she said.

'They're criminals who were facing death by digestion; I don't think gratitude was high on their list of priorities.'

'Maybe not, but if they get away they'll get to the treasure before us.'

'I don't think so,' I replied. 'They're obviously not in league with the giant, even though I suspect they thought they could talk him around when they climbed the beanstalk. I think their first priority will be to get out of here and report back to whoever hired them.'

'And who do you think that is?'Miss Muffet asked.

'I'm not sure yet, but, as our brothers in blue like to say, "I'm following a definite line of enquiry."'

'So you do know who's behind this?'

'I have a fair idea, but I don't want to say just yet; I need some more information first.' I'd finally started to piece together the case based on what I'd seen and heard over the past twenty-four hours and was pretty sure I knew who was behind it all – but I could still be wrong.

What? I hear you say, Harry Pigg wrong? I know it's highly unlikely, but I just needed to be certain – assuming I could get out of here alive. And that was my current priority; solving the case could wait a while longer, until I'd evaded an angry giant with non-selective carnivorous dietary habits and his mangy bunch of goblin guards. At least I knew Sinbad's fortune was definitely here somewhere – if the chicken and turkey were to be believed.

Now, I had to come up with another plan. I gathered the others around and briefed them on our current situation. 'We're on top of a table that's thirty feet off the ground; any second now, Neringus will probably be back for his soup and sandwiches and will be a bit miffed when he discovers the main ingredients have flown the coop. His state of mind probably won't be appeased in any way when he sees that we're out of the bowl, so we need to get out of here soonest.' Nods of agreement all round.

As it turned out, getting down off the desk wasn't too difficult. A combination of the rope Miss Muffet and Jack had used to rescue us, together with the rubber bands, allowed us to climb down without too much difficulty – although in Basili's case it became more like a bungee jump than a descent. It took three bounces before we were able to snag him and lower him safely to the carpet.

'Now what?' whispered Jack.

'Now we head for the wall and try to keep out of sight until we get to the door,' I replied. 'Everyone, follow me.'

The four of us crept along by the skirting until we reached the door which, thankfully, the giant hadn't closed when he left the room. It was a small break, but one we were grateful for. Over the past hour we had done more acrobatics than an average circus troupe and I wasn't keen to add any new tweaks to our act. Motioning the others to stop, I peeked around the door frame. The landing appeared empty. It stretched ahead, doors on both sides and the stairs to the lower level at the far end. The trip back to the front door would be an endurance test.

I turned to the others. 'Looks like it's clear. Let's go. And remember, stay close to the wall.'

Miss Muffet tapped me on the shoulder. 'Remind me again, where are we going?'

'The plan is to get out of here. It's too dangerous to hang around, so I suggest we make for the front door and head back to the beanstalk,' I said.

'And then what? Do you really think that Sinbad's fortune will be here when we come back – assuming we do come back?'

I looked pointedly at Jack Horner. 'It may not be, but my priority now is to get the others back to Grimmtown before they come to any harm. If that means we don't find the loot, then so be it. Ready?' I ran out of the door and, tight to the wall, began to make my way down the landing towards the stairs. I'd only taken a few steps when I heard music wafting up from the ground floor. From the sound of it, the harp was singing for her metaphorical supper while the giant applauded enthusiastically. It was like listening to a thunderstorm. Then another thunderstorm, as metaphorical as the harp's supper, set off lightning bolts in my head. It was something the harp had said and I'd only now registered the significance of it. Considering the giant's innate hostility to any kind of visitor, I was fairly sure the only person in this whole scenario who'd be able to visit Neringus's castle without fearing for their life was the mastermind behind the whole caper. All I needed to do now was to escape and unmask them – and see how I keep referring to the villain in the plural? – that's just to keep you guessing, assuming you haven't figured it out yet.

17

The Axeman Cometh

The stairs proved to be easier than I expected; then again we were going down. Even Jack was able to hang off the edge and drop to the lower step each time. It took a long and tiring time to get to the bottom and by the time we did we were barely able to stand. Between us and freedom was a huge lobby, a guard hut, a drawbridge, a longer walk across the clouds, an immigration post (hopefully still unoccupied) and a short beanstalk descent to our balloon. I just hoped we wouldn't collapse from exhaustion before we got to it.

Basili had dropped to his knees. 'Oh, Mr Harry, I do not think I am making it to our balloon. You must be leaving me here and be going on without me.'

Before I could give my heroic reply about never leaving a man or ex-genie behind, Jack fell down beside him. 'Me neither,' he gasped, 'but please don't leave me here and go on without me.'

Miss Muffet bent over, struggling for breath and put her hands on my shoulders for support. 'They're right. I'm tired too. We need an alternative option, otherwise we'll never get back.'

Privately, I was glad they were exhausted; I was too. I just didn't want to be the first to admit it. 'Okay, find someplace to hide while I see what I can come up with,' I ordered. I wasn't sure what I was looking for, but I had to find something and fast. If the giant or one of his goons spotted us we were toast – or maybe soup.

I scuttled away and, still hugging the wall, made my way to the room adjoining the giant's music room. The door was slightly open so I was able to peer through the crack and take a look around. From what I could see, I was looking at the dining room. A huge table and chairs dominated the centre and pictures of Neringus and the rest of what looked to be a very ugly family indeed adorned (if adorned could be said to be the correct word) the walls. My quick examination revealed nothing that might be of assistance and I was wondering if I'd find anything useful when I became aware of a raucous noise coming from the far end of the lobby. It wasn't loud enough, or even sophisticated enough, to belong to a giant and sounded like whoever was making it was having a good time.

The goblins! Of course; the giant's guards had to have someplace to live while they were off duty. They were hardly going to commute up and down from Grimmtown on a daily basis – and they had to have some way to get quickly to and from any rogue beanstalks that might suddenly appear in the giant's domain. Imbued with a fresh, albeit faint, sense of hope, I headed towards the source of the noise, alert for any stray goblins.

As I got close I could see the source of the goblin revelry was a small wooden cottage, nestling snugly under the stairs out of sight. I wasn't too bothered about checking it out, though. Oh, no, all I needed was the rat-drawn cart that was secured to a post outside the cottage. Now, in normal circumstances, the fact that the vehicle was drawn by two giant rats that seemed to be all teeth, fur and drool might be a cause for concern, but, in my current circumstances, I couldn't really afford to be choosy. It was the cart or nothing. At least, being goblins, they hadn't bothered with any guards outside the cottage. This wasn't really carelessness; if I had been them, I wouldn't have been too worried about anyone breaking in and stealing anything belonging to me. It was a giant's castle after all – who'd be mad enough? Apart, that is, from me.

Oh, so carefully, I sneaked up to the rats and, mindful of the teeth, gently untied the reins all the while muttering, 'easy boys' and 'there, there'. I know they weren't horses, but I wasn't sure how exactly to address a giant rat. All I wanted to ensure was that they didn't decide I looked like a very appetizing meal. Fortunately, either I didn't look appetizing or they'd already been fed because I managed to undo the reins and step up onto the driver's seat without any difficulty. The difficulty, of course, happened immediately afterwards. No sooner was I on the cart than the door to Goblin HQ opened and one of them came out for a smoke or a stroll or something. It didn't take him long to spot that his personal fleet was being hijacked.

'Oi, you,' he bellowed. 'Get down off that. It don't belong to you.'

I didn't stop to discuss the ethics of robbery when in a desperate situation. I just grabbed the whip from the holder beside me, cracked it over the rats' heads and yelled 'mush, mush'. The rats bounded forward, almost toppling me off balance as the cart lurched beneath me. I heaved on the reins and tried to force the rats over to where the others waited. For a few seconds it was rat against pig; they wanted to go one way, I another. Bit by bit I managed to force them in the direction I wanted and once they saw I was stronger (and had a whip), they caved in and raced away towards the foot of the stairs.

'Everyone, get ready to jump,' I roared at the others. 'I'm not sure I can get this thing to stop.' To their credit, when they saw me bearing down on them in a rat-powered cart ,they didn't bat an eyelid. In fairness, they'd seen so many strange things that day this was just one more – and one that they could grasp.

I pulled back on the reins, shouting, 'Whoa boys' at the same time (well, in fairness, my only exposure to animal-drawn vehicles was what I'd seen watching Westerns, so my grasp of commands was based on what I'd heard cowboys say). The rats didn't really 'whoa', but they did slow down enough to allow my friends to clamber in the back. Once they were safely on board, I cracked the whip once more – now that I was getting the hang of it – and the carriage raced towards the drawbridge.

'Faster, Harry,' Jack shouted into my ear. 'The goblins are coming after us.'

True, but as they were on foot, they had no chance of catching us. I was far more concerned about those in the guard hut at the drawbridge, who, even now, were swarming out. Either the card game was over or they'd been alerted to our presence.

'Goblins ahead,' I roared. 'I'm going to need help up here. Anything in the back we can use.'

'We're onto it,' Miss Muffet replied. Seconds later she appeared on the seat beside me.

'Well?' I said hopefully.

"There isn't much by way of weapons, but there is lots of fruit and veg – most of it rotten. It's not great, but,' she hefted a head of cabbage in her hand, 'it's better than nothing. Okay, everyone, grab something and prepare to pelt.' There was a scuffling from behind as the others burrowed into the rotting pile to find the best weapon.

Out in front, the goblins were forming a ragged line and bringing weapons to bear. Seconds later they were running for cover as a barrage of rotten tomatoes, cabbages and what looked like a very solid head of cauliflower ('that one was mine,' Jack yelled gleefully) rained down on them. To tell the truth, I think the vicious snapping of the giant rats probably had more of an impact, but, either way, it cleared them out of our path. The cart bounced across the drawbridge and onto the road that led back to the beanstalk. Surely nothing could prevent our escape now.

Of course, as soon as I think something like that, inevitably some new obstacle presents itself in our way – or in this case, right behind us. From the music room, I heard the urgent shouts of the harp as she alerted her master to our escape. Damn, she had seen us.

This was followed by a bellowing like an explosion and the giant roared, 'FEE, FIE, FOE, FUM, I SMELL THE BLOOD OF AN...UM...AH...PIG, TWO HUMANS AND SOMETHING ELSE. BE THEY ALIVE OR BE THEY DEAD, I'LL GRIND THEIR BONES TO MAKE SOUP, BREAD, A NICE PIE AND SOME LEFTOVERS FOR SUPPER.'

I hoped that if he did catch us that I would be dead before he decided to use us for some cookery, though my priority was to make sure we weren't actually caught at all. I cracked the whip once more trying, to get as much speed as I could out of the rats. To be fair, they were tearing along the road at a fair lick; I just didn't think they'd be able to outrun the giant with his huge strides.

The ground shook as the giant started to run.

'He's catching up,' Miss Muffet's voice was on the edge of panic. 'Can't you go any faster?'

'I probably could, but the rats can't,' I shouted over my shoulder. 'Is there anything left you can use to slow him down?'

'It's fruit, Harry, not a tactical nuke.'

'Well, throw it at him anyway. Maybe it'll distract him.' I know, it was a stupid suggestion but it was the best I could come up with.

'No, wait.' Jack had decided to enter the conversation. 'I've got a brilliant idea. Just do what I do.'

Unable to look at what was going on behind or risk crashing the cart, I kept my eyes firmly on the road ahead, hoping that Jack's idea would work.

'Everyone, throw the fruit on the road in front of the giant, maybe he'll slip on it.' I could hear the desperate enthusiasm in Jack's voice, but, as ideas went, it wasn't the worst. Mind you, it wasn't the best either. The chances of Neringus slipping were...

'Whoops, there he goes,' Jack shouted. This was followed immediately by a loud crash as the giant hit the ground. The vibrations bumped the cart into the air and it bounced around wildly for a few seconds before I could get control once more.

'What's he doing now?' I asked, wondering if Jack's idea had given us enough time.

'He's getting up, but very slowly,' Miss Muffet said. 'He looks a bit dazed.' She paused for a second. 'Oh, no. He's after us again, but at least he doesn't seem to be moving as fast.'

Onwards we raced, pursued by the stunned giant. From the confused commentary in the back of the cart, he seemed to be gaining, just not as speedily as before.

Ahead, I could see the tip of the beanstalk getting nearer and nearer; I hoped we'd make it in time, but, just when I thought we were going to do it, I noticed that the rats' pace had begun to flag. In fairness, I'd driven them hard all the way from the castle and they hadn't let me down. By now their tongues were dangling from their mouths and their fur was covered in sweat. They were probably on the point of collapse and I couldn't really blame them; they hadn't much left to give.

'How near is he?' I roared.

'He's almost on us,' Miss Muffet replied. 'Can't you go any faster?'

'The rats have had it. There's nothing in the tank.'

'There's got to be something you can do.'

The rats were almost at walking pace now. 'There's only one thing for it,' I said.

'What?' exclaimed the others in unison, clearly expecting another great idea.

'We get out and run,' I replied, to groans of disappointment. That was a clear signal my idea didn't entirely meet with the approval of the group. Then again, some of us weren't exactly built for running; at a pinch – and this was most definitely a pinch – we might just be able to manage a brisk walk. 'Like, now.' I jumped off the cart and ran – well, lumbered – towards the beanstalk. Following my example, the others followed, Jack in the lead, then Miss Muffet and, at the back, a less-than-mobile Basili.

Freed of their passengers, the rats lurched sideways off the road, dragging the cart behind them. It was a small diversion, but might just be enough. As the giant pounded after it, we raced towards the beanstalk, arriving just as Neringus realised his mistake and changed direction again – only this time straight at us.

Without looking, I jumped straight down through the cloud-cover, hoping that the balloon hadn't drifted away. It hadn't and, as an added bonus, I had a soft landing on the bodies of the goblins we'd dumped there earlier. Pausing only to throw them out of the basket (and onto a large nearby leaf – I'm not that cruel, you know), I undid the mooring rope just as the others fell into the balloon behind me.

'How fast can this thing drop?' I asked Miss Muffet.

She pushed me aside. 'As fast as ballast and hot air will allow. Now let me drive.'

The balloon drifted sideways, away from the beanstalk, and, as Miss Muffet made adjustments, slowly began to descend back towards Grimmtown.

'Can't it go any faster?' I asked.

'Give me a chance,' she replied. 'I have to make some very precise calculations.'

'Maybe if I climbed back out there and pulled off one of those patches, would that work?'

'Unless I get it right very soon, you might just have to.'

Bluff called, I skulked back over to the basket's edge and looked up. As I did so, a huge foot planted itself on the beanstalk and, seconds later, the rest of the giant followed, climbing down after us, his eyes focused on the not-so-rapidly-descending balloon.

I looked over at Miss Muffet once more. 'I know, I know,' she said. 'You don't have to tell me. He's up there isn't he?'

I nodded.

'Okay, time for extreme measures.' She pulled a cable and the parachute valve at the top of the balloon opened, releasing hot air. The balloon began to drop more rapidly.

'That's more like it,' I said.

'Just keep an eye on how fast we're dropping,' Miss Muffet replied. 'I'd prefer a gentle landing as opposed to a crashing one.'

'You're okay; the ground's a good bit away yet.'

'And we're moving towards it a little bit faster than I'd like,' Miss Muffet pointed out. 'And what are we going to do when we land? The giant won't be far behind us.'

Her point was well made. Think, Harry, think.

When the obvious solution struck me, I slapped myself on the forehead for taking so long to come up with it. I grabbed my mobile and made a call to Ezekiel Clubfoote. Zeke supplied me with whatever equipment I needed – and could afford. If he didn't have it, it probably didn't exist, and in the past I'd asked for some very strange stuff indeed. This time, however, my request was a simple one. Zeke listened, told me he could provide it and it'd be there when we landed. I thanked him and hung up.

'I have a plan,' I said. 'But it's contingent on getting to the ground before he does.' I jerked my trotter in the giant's direction.

Miss Muffet looked at Neringus, took a quick glance over the edge of the basket and announced that it would be a close thing – which wasn't exactly what I was hoping for.

I followed her example and looked down. A large crowd had gathered around the base of the beanstalk, all of them looking up at the bizarre chase going on above. Apart from the usual crowd of rubberneckers, I could see the police, operatives from Beanstalk Control in their bright green uniforms and, unless I was very much mistaken, most of the guests from the B&B. I wasn't surprised by the gathering; even by Grimmtown standards, a hot-air balloon being chased down a beanstalk by a giant wasn't something they saw every day. Although most of the onlookers were a safe distance away, of course, there was also a smaller, more gormless, crowd closer to the base of the beanstalk looking up at us in fascination. Unless they got out of the way soon, they risked being crushed by the rapidly descending balloon.

I waved my arms frantically. 'Get out of the way, you idiots.' Being the polite citizens they were, they happily waved back at me, seemingly oblivious of their impending demise.

'Morons,' I muttered. 'Well, if they can't be bothered to listen, anything that happens to them won't be on my head.' Which was true, it'd be on theirs – and in a matter of seconds, judging by our rate of descent. Miss Muffet was right: it was going to be close. The small sea of faces below grew closer and closer and it would have been funny in other circumstances to see the way their expressions changed from bland looking-up to the sudden realization that they were in imminent danger of death. This was quickly followed by a scattering of bodies and a crash as the balloon hit the ground recently vacated by the idiot spectators.

I didn't waste any time checking everyone was okay, I just hurdled over the basket's edge and roared, 'Did anyone leave a package for me?'

Almost immediately, Queenie Harte and Mr Zingiber struggled forward carrying a large trunk between them. 'Is this what you're looking for?' the gingerbread man grunted.

'I expect so,' I said, as they gratefully dropped the trunk at my feet. I quickly undid the large clasp and opened it. 'Oh, Zeke,' I whispered, as I looked inside. 'You've excelled yourself this time.' Turning back to the balloon, I yelled at the others to get out of the basket as fast as they could. With Neringus almost within grabbing distance they didn't need any encouragement.

'Everyone stand back, this beanstalk is about to come down,' I shouted.

'Cool,' I heard Jack say. 'Have you an axe, just like the Giantkiller?'

'Axe be damned,' I said grimly, heaving a large chainsaw out of the trunk and revving it up. 'I don't believe in wasting my time and energy.' With the last remnants of my strength, I strode over to the beanstalk and held the chainsaw against the trunk. Bits of wood sprayed in all directions as the saw bit in. Above, the giant saw what was happening and stopped climbing down. Once I saw I had his attention, I pulled the chainsaw away and looked up at him.

'Now, I'm not normally a betting man,' I said, trying to sound more confident than I felt, 'but if I was to guess, I'd say I could cut this baby down before you got to the ground.'

'You wouldn't,' Neringus said; a trifle uncertainly, I thought.

I revved up the saw once more. It made a very reassuring roar. 'Try me.'

Behind me the crowd had begun to chant, 'Cut it down! Cut it down!'

'See,' I said. 'Even the crowd is on my side.'

'What do you want?' the giant asked. Good. At last he was starting to see sense.

'I want you to head back up to your lovely castle in the clouds and not bother me again,' I said, swinging the chainsaw towards the beanstalk for effect.

The giant flinched. 'That's all?'

'No. Did you really think that would be all?' Now that I had him where I wanted him, relatively speaking, I had to make the most of it. 'Some nice people from Beanstalk Control, along with representatives of our police service, will probably be along to pay you a visit and relieve you of Sinbad's treasure, which as we know, doesn't actually belong to you.'

'But I was only minding it for him,' the giant stammered. 'He asked me to.'

'And now you can make sure that it's returned to its rightful owners, seeing as Sinbad won't be needing it for quite some time yet. Do we understand each other?'

Neringus nodded. 'Good,' I said. 'Now toddle back up there and leave us alone, or else...' I revved the chainsaw up one last time. I must say, I quite liked the noise it made.

Fearful of plummeting out of a chopped-down beanstalk, the giant climbed quickly away, to the accompaniment of the cheers and applause of the onlookers. Soon he was out of sight and hopefully back where he belonged. Since that he was out of our harm's way, I handed the chainsaw to one of Beanstalk Control's representatives. 'I know it's an unlicensed growth and needs to come down, but, before you cut it down, the cops will need to go up there. That guy's been hiding Sinbad's treasure since he went to jail, so it needs to be recovered and returned to the original owners.'

The BC rep looked confused, but nodded anyway; he probably didn't know what else to do.

'And now,' I announced to the crowd with a flourish, 'I just need to wrap this case up once and for all so, if the police would be kind enough to escort all the B&B's guests into the house and make sure they don't try to escape,' I did a quick headcount just to be sure everyone was still there, 'I'll explain everything.' Then another thought struck me. 'And if one or two of the police could remain here, I suspect that two more refugees from above may be arriving at any second. If they do, assuming they haven't become a giant's nourishing bowl of soup, they're to be arrested immediately.'

18

A Surprise Ending

Once everyone was sitting down in the lounge, I stood beside the fireplace and began. 'Now, this may come as a surprise to you all, but I'm not actually Harriet du Crêpe, PA to Alain Schmidt-Heye, but Harry Pigg, Grimmtown's foremost detective.' I didn't get the gasps of astonishment I was expecting. Maybe it was the remnants of the make-up, which was still liberally smeared across my face.

'Miss Muffet hired me to find out who was behind the spider infestation in her house. Initially, I believed someone was trying to put her out of business, but after some rather brilliant detective work, I came to the conclusion that the real reason was that someone wanted to lay their hands on her father's fortune, which they believed was hidden somewhere in the house. You see, Miss Muffet's father is Sinbad the Sailor, whom I'm sure you've all heard of.' This revelation was greeted with some gasps of amazement (now that was more like it) and muted nods. 'And this, though I'm reluctant to admit it, is where I made my first mistake.'

'Only the first?' asked Queenie, but I chose to ignore her cheap shot.

'You see, I didn't realise that Sinbad's treasure was never hidden in the house,' I continued. 'All that was actually here was the means to get to it.'

'The magic bean,' Jack shouted.

'Yes, Jack, the magic bean.' I said. 'Once that was found, thanks to some more superb detective work by yours truly, it led to the kingdom in the clouds and the actual location of the treasure.'

Miss Muffet stood up. 'Okay, Harry, we know all this now. What we need to find out is who's behind it.'

'Patience, good lady; all will be revealed shortly.'

She sat down once more, an impatient look on her face.

'It seemed clear to me that one of the guests had to be masterminding the whole caper. The question remained, which of you was it?'

This was greeted with indignant harrumphs and denials from the guests.

'For reasons I won't go into, I eliminated Mr Winkie from my enquiries early on. Mr and Mrs Spratt seemed to be on the level too, so I focused my attentions on the remaining guests, all of whom had something to hide.' Much guilty shifting about followed this statement. 'Yes, all of you.'

'I made one fatal assumption at this point: as I knew Licken and Lurkey of old, I hadn't considered the possibility that they might be involved. Of course, being both stupid and short of cash, they made ideal stooges for the brains behind the operation. All they had to do was keep an eye out for any sign of where the magic bean might be hidden and report back.'

'But report back to whom?' Miss Muffet asked, clearly puzzled. 'How did you know it wasn't Licken and Lurkey?'

'Once our fowl friends recognised me last night, they must have immediately told their boss who I was and what they thought I was up to. When I found the magic bean, someone knocked me out and grabbed it,' I said. 'The last thing I saw before I blacked out was a hand picking up the box – not a wing, a hand. This obviously meant there was a human involved.

'Once the magic bean was located and triggered, it became obvious where the treasure was, but this also presented a problem, as giants don't obviously like uninvited guests and it would have taken too long for a visitor to get an official visa – especially for an unapproved beanstalk. Therefore, whoever wanted to get their hands on the treasure needed to act fast and come up with a good reason to visit Neringus's kingdom.' I was getting to the good stuff now and I could sense the growing anticipation in my audience – at least, in those of them that weren't involved. 'And what better reason than to repair the giant's most treasured possession.'

Jack jumped to his feet. 'The magic harp; she was all scratched and she said she was due for repair and revarnishing.'

'Yes, Jack, Licken and Lurkey were sent up there with explicit instructions to damage the harp. As she was the giant's favourite and as he probably couldn't bear to listen to her complain about the damage, he needed her to be attended to urgently, and who better to do it than someone who's familiar with working on and restoration of the most delicate of wooden antiques and carvings.' I pointed my finger at Pietro Nocchio. 'I'm, of course, referring to you, Mr Nocchio.'

The wooden man jumped to his feet. 'That eez ridiculous; I've never 'eard anything so absurd 'een my whole life.'

'Working with puppets, I'm sure you have,' I replied. 'They're not known for their common sense.'

'That eez an outrageous accusation,' he shouted. 'I am only 'ere to meet some puppet dealers.'

'Of course you are; and no doubt you knew nothing about Sinbad or his treasure, did you?'

'Absolutely not! Before I came 'ere, I 'ad never heard of Sinbad, heez treasure or George Etto.'

'And who said anything about Etto?' I asked, smiling, knowing that I had him. 'I don't recall mentioning his name during any of this.'

Nocchio looked at me, horror-stricken. By mentioning Sinbad's former cellmate, he'd effectively sealed his fate. He sat at the table, his head in his hands.

'I thought no one would cotton on. I was dreenking in the Blarney Tone weeth some buddies and we 'eard thees Etto guy ramble on about how 'e 'ad 'eard Sinbad talking een hees sleep. At first I didn't pay much attention, but when he said something about the secret to his treasure being hidden een the house, then I got very interested. I bought heem some more drinks and 'e kept telling the same story: somewhere in thees house was the key to get to Sinbad's fortune. All I 'ad to do was find eet.

'I thought that by scaring Miss Muffet away, I'd have the place to myself. I couldn't believe eet when thees bunch of cheapskates and nostalgia junkies just wouldn't leave, so I 'ired Licken and Lurkey to help me look around. Once they realised who you really were, I figured that eef anyone could find the secret it'd be you.'

I preened when he said this.

'The rest you know. I was so close to getting up there. Once I did, I planned to make a deal with the giant and give eem some of the treasure. With Sinbad in jail for the foreseeable future, I figured I'd be long gone before 'e found out.' Nocchio sighed heavily and extended his arms. Seconds later he was led away in cuffs.

Chalk up another success to the Third Pig Detective Agency. But there was one last aspect of the case to consider.

'Oh, and considering what I heard at breakfast this morning, you might also want to talk to Mr Nimble here,' I said. 'I suspect he's also involved, as the man who'd help dispose of this massive fortune to collectors all over the world in return for some highly lucrative commission, as well as being the man who, disguised as an orc, organised for the supply of the spiders.'

Nimble stood up and blustered, 'This is an outrage. I won't stand for this slur on my good character.'

Miss Muffet walked up behind him and pushed him back down into his seat. 'Sit,' she ordered. 'I bet Nocchio will be quite happy to make a deal in return for telling us exactly how much you were involved.'

As she spoke there came the sound of wings beating from outside, followed immediately by a loud and indignant squawking. 'Ah,' I said, 'I do believe Licken and Lurkey have returned to ground level and have met their welcoming committee.'

After the police had escorted Nocchio and Nimble away, Miss Muffet rushed over and hugged me. 'Thank you, Harry,' she said. 'I don't know how I can ever repay you.'

'It's okay,' I said. 'Just pay me out of the reward money.'

'Reward money?'

'Some of the stuff Sinbad stole over the years is very valuable indeed. I fully expect there'll be a reward for its safe recovery and as the magic bean was found in your house and the beanstalk is on your property, I think you have a reasonable first claim on the loot. Spend it wisely. As a first step, I'd suggest a pest extermination service. Although I suspect that Mr Frogg Prince might be only too delighted to take the spiders off your hands. In fact, being a frog, he may very well double up as an exterminator considering the length of his tongue.'

'I think you're right. Thanks again, Harry.'

'My pleasure. But before we go, there are a few things I'd like to get answers to.' I looked at Thomas Piper. 'What's your story? You haven't taken your eyes off Miss Muffet since you arrived.'

Piper shuffled his feet guiltily. 'It's nothing sinister; I was watching out for her on her father's instructions. Once he got word of the spiders he asked me to move in and make sure nothing happened to her.'

'And what's your connection to Sinbad?' I asked.

'Let's just say we worked together in the past,' Piper replied.

'You mean you were part of his gang,' I said.

'I can't comment on that; however, I'm sure Mr El Muhfte will be suitably grateful that this situation has been resolved.'

'How grateful?' I asked hopefully, figuring he might throw some cash in my direction as a reward.

'Alas, now that his treasure has been recovered, actual monetary recompense might not be as forthcoming.'

Dammit, I'd shot myself in the foot there.

'And as for you, Miss Harte,' I said, turning to face her. 'You're about as likely a GBI agent as I am. I saw through you almost immediately; what gives?'

Queenie gave a rueful shrug. 'Sorry about that. I really didn't mean any harm. I was only here on behalf of the Grimmtown Spider Preservation Society. I'm a private detective too, and like you I was trying to find out what had happened.'

'But why the fake ID and the GBI story; wouldn't it have been just as easy to say who you really were?'

'This coming from someone who disguised himself as a woman in order to solve the case?'

'*Touché*,' I said. 'But remember who it was that solved the case.' Well, I couldn't let a gloating opportunity go by, now, could I?

'Come on,' I said to Jack and Basili, 'our work here is done. Dinner is on me.'

Together we walked out of the lounge, down the hall to the front door. Just as we were about to open it, it swung inwards and three burly policemen entered followed by a large fly dressed in a very smart grey suit.

'You're too late,' I said. 'You've just missed the others. They're probably on their way to the station right now.'

'Harry Pigg?' said the leading cop.

'That's me,' I replied, extending my trotter. To my surprise, he snapped a handcuff around it.

'You're under arrest for murder,' he said, his face expressionless.

I looked at him in shock. 'This is a joke, right? Who put you up to it? DI Jill?'

'This is no joke, sir. You're under arrest for the murder of Geoffrey Coque-Robben. Please extend your other arm.'

I realised that this wasn't a joke after all. 'You must be mistaken. I haven't killed anyone,' I said, as the handcuffs were snapped onto my other trotter.

'Sir, please, if you'll just accompany us to the station.' The other two policemen grabbed an arm each and escorted me out the door and towards a police car that was parked on the road outside the B&B.

'What's going on, Harry?' Jack cried. 'What are they doing?'

'It's okay, Jack, I'm sure it's some kind of mistake. We'll get it sorted at the police station.'

'It's no mistake, sir,' said the policeman to my left. 'We have a witness.'

'What witness? Who?' This was becoming more unreal by the minute. How could anyone have possibly seen me commit a murder I obviously hadn't done.

The fly, who up to now had been maintaining a discreet distance, stepped forward.

'I,' said the fly. 'I saw him die, with my little eye; and you were the one that killed him.'

Bob Burke

The End

The Third Pig Detective Agency will return
in
The I Said the Fly Mystery

Acknowledgements

This has been a strange year (to put it mildly). Unexpected things happened and I truly became aware of the meaning of the word family. The word 'Thanks' doesn't even begin to express my gratitude for the support of my wife, Gemma, my three boys, Ian, Adam and Stephen, my parents, brothers and sister. Here's looking at you, folks.

Gem, words can't express...

Ian (assuming you're actually awake and out of bed), I truly appreciate your offer and the fact that you volunteered immediately.

Adam, you've had a great year. Cool stuff has happened and you're beginning to realise your potential. I sense great things (or a disturbance in the Force or it might be just indigestion).

Stephen, think of this as a time machine of sorts. As I write, Munster are in the HC quarter-finals. By the time you read it, they may be champions – or may have been defeated on the way. Who can say (right now)? Hopefully, we'll get to see (have seen!!) them on the rest of their journey.

As always, my gratitude goes to my agent, Svetlana, and to Scott and Corinna at The Friday Project for the editing and other publishy type stuff that ensured this story actually got to print.

Harry Pigg doesn't believe in thanking anyone other than himself so his acknowledgements will be conspicuous by their absence this time around.